ISBN 978-1-330-06346-0
PIBN 10016499

This book is a reproduction of an important historical work. Forgotten Books uses
state-of-the-art technology to digitally reconstruct the work, preserving the original format
whilst repairing imperfections present in the aged copy. In rare cases, an imperfection in
the original, such as a blemish or missing page, may be replicated in our edition. We do,
however, repair the vast majority of imperfections successfully; any imperfections that
remain are intentionally left to preserve the state of such historical works.

1 MONTH OF
FREE
READING

at

www.ForgottenBooks.com

By purchasing this book you are eligible for one month membership to ForgottenBooks.com, giving you unlimited access to our entire collection of over 700,000 titles via our web site and mobile apps.

To claim your free month visit:

www.forgottenbooks.com/free16499

Similar Books Are Available from
www.forgottenbooks.com

LIFE IMPRISONMENT

—— vs. ——

THE DEATH PENALTY

———————

To the Honorable Members of the Senate and Lower
House of the Fifty-eighth General Assembly
and to the Chairman and Members
of the Judiciary Commit-
tees Thereof.

———————

THE BRIEF OF DUKE C. BOWERS, Et Als., Advocates

——ON——

*Senate Bill No. 242 and House Bill No. 235, Entitled "An
Act to Abolish the Death Penalty in the State of Tennessee,
and to Substitute Life Imprisonment Therefor."*

HISTORY OF CAPITAL PUNISHMENT.

In the early stages of society the man committing homicide was killed by the "Avenger of Blood" on behalf of the family of the man killed, and not as representing the authority of the State. That was the custom for centuries, till the mischief of this practice was mitigated by the establishment of cities of refuge, and in pagan and Christian times of the recognizing of the sanctuary of the temple and the churches. In the laws of Khamurobi, King of Babylon (2285-2241 B. C.) the death penalty was imposed for many offenses; the modes of execution specially mentioned are, drowning, burning and impalement.

See Capital Punishment, Vol. 5, Enc. Britanica.

Draco, the first compiler of the Penal Code of Greece, made death the penalty for all offenses. When asked why he did so, replied: "The least offenses deserve death, and I can impose no worse for the higher crimes."

Under the Mosaic Code the law of vengeance was personified in the then prevailing doctrine of *"EYE FOR AN EYE, AND A TOOTH FOR A TOOTH,"* in many instances that rule being carried out literally. In the dark ages of the United Kingdom, under the rule of the Saxon and Danish Kings, the modes of capital punishment most common were: "Hanging, beheading, drowning, burning, stoning, and precipitation from rocks." William the Conquerer would not permit the execution of the death sentence by hanging but by mutilation. (5 Vol. Enc. Britanica.)

Death was the penalty for the most trivial offenses; for example, the cutting of a tree or poaching deer. In 1800 there were over 200 capital crimes in Great Britain and 180 in 1819. Men were hung and quartered for offenses which now would be regarded as misdemeanors, while the learned clergy and statesmen looked on with approval and applause. During the reign of

Henry the VIII, 72,000 persons were executed. The first allevi ation came from the extension of the benefit of clergy to all persons who could read the "Neck-verse" (Ps. Li. 5, 1).

"At the end of the eighteenth century the criminal laws of all Eirope were ferocious and indiscriminate," says the author of "Capital Punishment," in Vol. 5, page 279, Enclycopedia Britanica, in its administration of capital punishment for almost all grave crimes,   . .   yet such forms of crime were far more numerous than they are now." The best blood of England drenched the execution block, and "Kech," the legal executioner, became more infamous than Rob Roy, the bandidt. Death was a panacea for all ills.

The States of our Union adopted the common law of England replete with capital offenses, but Tennessee, by statute, has finally limited the number, in practice at least, to two, murder and rape; but the statute names other offenses, and hanging is the mode of execution.

In Belgium no execution has taken place since 1863; in Finland since 1824; in Holland since 1860, and was totally abolished in 1870. No executions in Norway since 1876, abolished in 1905; abolished in Portugal in 1867; in Roumania in 1864. Russia abolished capital punishment, except for military offenses, in 1750, but later restored it for a short period, only to again abolish it in 1907. Only 7 out of 22 Cantons in Switzerland have it, and Italy revoked the law in 1888.

In the United States the number of capital crimes has been reduced in recent years to only four, and the following States have abolished it: Maine, in 1876, restored it in 1883, but again repealed the law in 1887 on the recommendation of the Governor of said State; Rhode Island, in 1853; Wisconsin, in 1853, and Kansas, in 1901, but there have been no legal executions in Kansas since 1872; Michigan in 1847.

BRIEF AND ARGUMENT.

It is now proposed to repeal the law of blood and vengeance in Tennessee, and make life imprisonment the maximum punishment in said State.

The two main objects in enforcing our criminal laws are (a) to protect society, (b) to reform the criminal. Some would add a third reason for punishing criminals, namely, to punish the criminal himself, but in this day of brotherly love, when we are taught to love our enemies, and when charity and love have triumphed over vengeance and hatred no one would seriously insist that the State any more has the right to kill a man to avenge the death of his victim than has an individual.

Every man will agree with us on this one point: if social conditions will not be made worse by the abolition of the death penalty, then it should be abolished. The only way we have to determine this question is by taking the statistics from the States with and without the death penalty.

STATISTICAL ABSTRACT.

According to the mortality statistics compiled by the United States Bureau of Statistics, and published in 1912, in table 5, page 376, the number of homicides per 100,000 population for the eighteen States composing the registration area was as follows:

State.	1900	'01	'02	'03	'04	'05	'06	'07	'08	'09
California—										
Cities	..	..	..	..	..	..	..	9.0	13.2	10.6 10.2
Rural	..	..	..	..	..	..	..	6.8	8.3	12.1 9.8
Colorado—										
Cities	..	..	..	..	..	..	..	10.4	7.4	18.7 9.0
Rural	..	..	..	..	..	..	..	13.9	18.0	15.6 12.4
Connecticut—										
Cities	0.3	0.5	0.6	0.3	1.8	2.0	2.5	3.6	2.8	
Rural	..	..	..	0.9		0.9	1.5	1.7	3.7	5.1

— 4 —

Indiana—

Cities	1.1	2.4	2.0	1.4	3.1	4.8	5.7	7.0	9.1	8.0
Rural	1.5	0.5	0.6	1.2	0.7	2.7	3.0	3.6	2.9	2.7

Maine—

Cities	1.7	..	2.5	2.4	3.2	0.6	2.2	0.6	1.1	
Rural	1.7	1.6	0.3	1.0	..	2.0	0.4	1.6	1.4	1.1

Maryland—

Cities	..	..	..	..	..	..	4.7	7.3	3.8	3.4
Rural	..	..	..	..	..	..	2.3	2.6	3.9	3.8

Massachusetts—

Cities	0.7	1.1	1.3	1.3	1.5	1.5	1.8	2.7	2.6	2.5
Rural	1.2	1.3	0.6	0.7	0.3	0.4	0.6	0.4	1.9	2.3

Michigan—

Cities	0.7	1.1	1.5	1.4	1.0	0.9	1.3	3.2	4.1	2.2
Rural	0.7	1.6	1.2	1.3	1.0	0.5	1.0	1.7	2.2	2.2

New Hampshire—

Cities	..	..	..	..	..	1.2	1.2	..	0.6	1.7
Rural	0.4	0.4	..	..	0.8	0.4	2.8	..	0.8	1.2

New Jersey—

Cities	1.7	0.9	1.4	0.7	1.3	1.8	2.9	4.2	3.7	4.7
Rural	0.1	0.1	0.8	0.2	0.9	1.4	2.5	3.2	4.6	2.9

New York—

Cities	2.00	1.8	2.0	1.4	2.2	3.5	5.0	6.1	5.3	4.4
Rural	0.2	0.4	0.3	0.5	0.5	0.6	1.8	3.3	3.6	3.3

Ohio—

Cities	..	..	..	..	..	..	..	..	..	7.4
Rural	..	..	..	..	..	..	..	..	..	2.8

Pennsylvania—

Cities	..	..	..	..	..	..	5.8	6.5	5.0	4.7
Rural	..	..	..	..	..	..	4.5	4.8	4.9	4.1

Rhode Island—

Cities	2.5	2.8	2.7	2.3	3.5	2.5	3.9	5.5	4.2	3.0
Rural	2.8	0.7	4.0	1.9	1.9	0.6	2.3	1.1	3.3	2.1

South Dakota—

Cities	..	..	..	..	..	..	..	..	7.4	7.2
Rural	..	..	..	..	..	..	2.1	2.6	3.8	2.2

Vermont—

Cities	..	..	..	..	2.0	2.0		3.9	3.8	3.8
Rural		0.3	0.3	0.3	0.3	2.0	1.0	1.3	2.3	3.8

Washington—

Cities ...	..	..	..	..	..	..	..	..	11.7	8.1
Rural .	..	..	..	..	..	..	..	..	6.3	4.2

Wisconsin—

Cities ..	..	..	..	..	..	..	..	..	3.1	1.9
Rural .	..	..	..	..	..	..	..	..	1.6	1.7

It will thus be seen by referring to the statistics quoted above that for the ten-year period, beginning with 1900, the average number of homicides in the States where capital punishment has been abolished per hundred thousand population was: Maine, 2.5; Michigan, 3.8; Rhode Island, 5; and for the two years, 1908 and 1909, for which Wisconsin reported her homicides, she averaged 4.1, but decreased in 1909 over the previous year. In some of the States where capital punishment prevailed we find that for a ten-year period, beginning with the year 1900, the average number of homicides per 100,000 population was: Indiana, 6.4; New Jersey, .4; New York, 4.8; and for the four years reported by Pennsylvania an average of 9.8. Ohio reports for the year 1900 only, giving 10.2; California for a four-year period shows twenty homicides per 100,000 population. While Massachusetts only shows an average of 2:57 for each 100,000 population, the increase in that State from 1905 to 1909 was 100 per cent. It will be further seen that California, Connecticut, Massachusetts, Indiana, New Jersey, New York, Pennsylvania and Vermont, where capital punishment obtains, and where it is enforced rigidly, shows an increase in the number of homicides for the period reported in the above statistics, while of the four States that have abolished the death penalty, only Michigan shows an increase, which is slight, but her general average for a ten-year period is less than either of the States that have retained the death penalty, with the exception of Vermont and New Hampshire: and that they have increased their homicide rate per annum continually, while Michigan shows a decrease in 1000 over the previous year. Besides, the record shows that the death penalty has been abolished in Vermont and New Hampshire by practice for twenty years.

The general average for the period reported in the above table of statistics for the four States where the death penalty has been revoked is 3.85 per 100,000 population, while for the States inflicting the death penalty, for the period reported, the general average is 8.25, or nearly 115 per cent greater. The average homicidal rate in Tennessee was five times greater than in either of the abolition States.

While we were unable to get the statistics on this question from Kansas, we are reliably informed that the number of homicides in that State per capita is comparatively small, and in a recent letter from the secretary of the present Governor of that State he informs us that the people there are universally pleased with the workings of the new law abolishing the death penalty, and that there is no disposition to restore capital punishment in that State. It will be remembered that there has never been a legal execution in that State since 1872, the Governors in their discretion failing to sign the death warrants at the end of one year's imprisonment, as the law required.

THE RESULTS OBTAINED IN FOREIGN COUN TRIES FROM THE ABOLITION OF THE DEATH PENALTY ARE NO LESS BENEFICIAL THAN IN OUR OWN STATES.

We take the following facts and statistics from Report No. 108 on capital crimes of the Fifty-fourth United States Congress, first session, printed January 22, 1896, by order of the House of Representatives

BELGIUM.—"The penalty of death has not been abolished in Belgium, but since 1866 it has not been executed. In order for one to appreciate the results, the following statistics are given: For the period from 1831 to 1890, in the first thirty-five years there were 321 capital condemnations, which was at the rate of 9.17 per year. In the twenty-five years following the cessation of executions there were 201, which was at the rate of 8.004, showing a decrease of 1.1696."

COSTA RICA.—"The results of the abolition of capital punishment for all offenses in Costa Rica are considered very favorable, this confirming public sentiment against capital punishment."

HATI.—"The Constitution of 1879 abolished the death penalty for political offenses. Since the period of said abolition political crimes have not been more frequent."

HOLLAND.—"There has been no increase of crime since the abolition of the death penalty."

ITALY.—"Since the abolition of the death penalty by the new Common Penal Code, which went into force January 1, 1890, the results obtained up to this present time have fully realized the expectations cherished by Parliament, by public opinion, and by students of criminal matters; that is to say, social security has not been disturbed or diminished by it, and consequently the conditions of high criminality have not been rendered worse."

NORWAY.—"Since 1874 it is made discretionary with the Courts, of death or hard labor for life, since which time a majority of the latter cases have been imposed, and no bad consequences, so far as public safety is concerned, have been observed."

PORTUGAL.—"The death penalty was abolished by the law

on the first of July, 1867, and the number of homicides to which this penalty was applied has diminished during the succeeding years."

SWITZERLAND.—"Since 1874 capital punishment has been abolished in fifteen of the twenty-two Cantons in Switzerland."

The only light we have to guide our advancing footsteps in enacting progressive legislation is the unerring light of experience. The record shows that the death penalty has been abolished in Michigan for sixty-six years; in Rhode Island for sixty-one years; in Wisconsin for sixty years; in Maine for thirty-seven years, and in Kansas by practice for about fifty years, and recently by statute, and yet those enlightened and progressive States have discovered no good reason for repealing these laws that have been in force for over a half century in most instances. That alone should be sufficient to convince that the abolition statutes have vindicated their existence. Besides, is it a mere coincidence that the States that have so long foregone the death penalty have less than one-half the number of homicides of the States that foster executions? Is it only a coincidence that homicides in Connecticut, Massachusetts, Vermont and New Hampshire have increased over previous years, while in their sister State of Maine, where life imprisonment is the highest penalty, the number of homicides have decreased in the same period. In 1909 the three States named above registered a total of homicides per 100,000 population as follows: Massachusetts, 4.8; Connecticut, 7.9; Vermont, 7.6, while in Maine, for the same period, 2.2 for the same ratio is shown.

Making further comparisons for the year 1909, we find registered homicides per 100,000 as follows: Michigan, 4.4; Wisconsin, 3.6, and Rhode Island, 5.1, as against the death penalty States as follows: Indiana, 10.7; Ohio, 10.2; Pennsylvania, 8.8; New York, 7.7; New Jersey, 7.6; Colorado, 21.4; California, 20; Maryland, 7.2; New Hampshire, 2.9; South Dakota, 9.4; Washington, 12.3. Can all of the above facts, so favorable to the

States that have abolished the death penalty, be attributed to mere chance?

In the same year the number of homicides per million people in the four abolition States was thirty-five; there were eighty-five in the death penalty States per million population. While in 1904, taking the whole United States, the ratio was 104.4 per million, while Maine, for the same year, registers 24 for each million inhabitants; Michigan, 20, and Rhode Island reports 51, or nearly one-half the general average for all the States.

The record further shows that from 1885 to 1904 homicides increased from 32.2 per million people to 104.4 for the same ratio. This is the face of the facts that capital punishment was in full force in every State in the Union but four or five.

The foreign States that have abolished it not only refuse to reinstate it, but the reports above quoted show that criminal conditions are in all instances as good, and in some reported better, than before the abolition of the death penalty.

After centuries of observation and experience, the learned Judges of England and America established a rule making a preponderance of evidence in civil cases the guide for themselves and juries in deciding questions of disputed facts. That is the only true rule. Then, have we not proven our case by an overwhelming preponderance of the proof? The evidence based on actual experience in our States and in foreign States is so near unanimous in favor of its abolition that it is a mere exception to a general rule that a fact militates against it.

BUT YOU ASK, "WHY WOULD LEGAL EXECUTIONS INCREASE CAPITAL CRIMES?

Because crime is largely a disease, and the demoralizing effect of a legal execution, and the example thus set by the State arouses the criminal natures and cheapens life in the estimation of the criminally inclined. Like begets like in this respect, as sure as night follows day. We cannot put it better than to quote from Mrs. Ella Wheeler Wilcox's beautiful poem on capital punishment:

"And last the people, frenzied or depressed
　　By sight or sound, or knowledge of the deed,
　Are wronged and injured by the law's effect;
　Crime follows executions; thought breeds thought,
　And as from thistledown new thistles spring,
　　So violent actions to disorders lead.
　That vengeful God of Hebraic Lore
　Has blocked the progress of the world too long.
　When Science seeks the cause, and Love the cure,
　Then crime will vanish from the human race."

Did you ever for a moment contemplate the moral wrecks, and devastation, and depravity that follow in the wake of war and of active armies? If anything, it is worse than the active warfare itself. Notwithstanding the guerrilla, if caught either by the Federal or Confederate, knew he would be shot by his captors, hundreds of formerly honorable men, or at least apparently so, became sutlers, ghouls, horse thieves and common robbers, and even little value or respect was placed on the virtue of our womanhood. Some of the women themselves were contaminated by the general moral stagnation, and many yielded to the degeneracy of the times. Human life, especially, became so cheap, in the estimation of the people, that murder became the rule instad of the exception.

The Government itself was engaged in the vocation of killing; the citizen, or at least the criminally inclined, put no higher value on life than his Government, and that is always true.

If we are to teach our citizenship that life is sacred we must not take it by law, nor even by law sanction it. As an example, the Quakers even refuse to go to war or for any reason take life, and they do not commit murders.

But you may say it deters others from committing crimes. If that is so, why have States that do not kill the smallest homicidal rate per capita? Why are such crimes increasing while the death penalty is being enforced?

If it deters to kill by hanging or electrocuting, it would certainly act as a much stronger deterrent if you would, as of old, torture and mutilate the murderer? You say that would be too cruel and barbarous and would demoralize the public and even brutalize men. Well, the majority of the people think inflicting the death penalty is too cruel and barbarous, and that the majority of people think so is proven by the fact that the great majority of the people want the condemned man cummuted to life imprisonment in each instance. Our descendants a century hence will look back on our legal executions with the same aversion and horror, and denounce us as we do our ancestors who burnt at the stake and mutilated the body of the condemned, or caused it to hang, for weeks, as a warning.

Dr. A. B. Martin, Dean of the Lebanon Law School of Cumberland University, gives a demonstrative illustration from his own observations, that hanging does not deter others from committing crimes.

A man was to be hanged on the Public Square, in Lebanon, Tenn., and the gallows was erected; two enterprising (we think infamously so) young men erected an arena around the scaffold, and on the day of the hanging were present and collected a great deal of money for their seats. Wtihin one and a half years both of the men were hanged for the same offense for which the victim that they had exploited was executed.

Some of the most shocking crimes follow closely the most notorious executions. For example, the Allens murdered Judge Massey and four others in the Court House at Hillsville, Va., while the papers of said State were heralding the news of the execution of the noted wife murderer, H. C. Beattie.

The assassination of Rosenthal in New York City followed closely on the heels of the execution of four men in New York State within one hour.

Instances are reported in which the spectators at a hanging in England for picking pockets committed the same offense for which the victim was being executed.

ANOTHER REASON WHY CAPITAL PUNISHMENT SHOULD BE ABOLISHED IS, THAT INNOCENT MEN ARE SOMETIMES EXECUTED.

Says Horace Greely: "I dread human frailty. Men are prejudiced, passionate, and too often irrational. Today they shout, 'Hosanna,' and tomorrow howl' 'Crucify him.' I would save them from the harsher consequences of their frenzy. Our Savior is by no means a solitary example of the unjust execution of the innocent and just. Socrates, Cicero, Sir Walter Raleigh, Algernon Sidney, John Huss, Michael Servetus, Louis XVI, the Duc d'Enghine, Marshal Ney, Riego, Nagi Sandor, Maximilian, are among the conspicuous instances of victims of the law of blood. We have recorded instances of innocent men convicted of murder on their own confession, of men convicted, sentenced and hanged for offenses whereof they were in no wise guilty. Men may suffer unjustly, even though death be stricken from the list of penalties, but to be imprisoned and stripped of property is quite endurable compared with the infliction of an ignominious death in the presence and for the delectation of a howling mob of exulting human brutes. So long as man is liable to error I would have him reserve the possibility of correcting his mistakes and redressing the wrong he is misled into perpetrating."

Mr. B. Paul Newman, writing for the Fortnightly Review, September, 1889, says: "Some time ago Sir James McIntosh, a most cool and dispassionate observer, declared that, taking a long period of time, one innocent man was hanged in every three years. The late Chief Baron Kelley stated as the result of his experience that from 1802 to 1840 no fwer than twenty-two innocent men had been sentenced to death, of whom seven were actually executd. These terrible mistakes are not confined to England; Mittermaier refers to cases of a similar kind in Ireland.

Italy, France, and Germany. In comparatively recent years ther have been several striking instances of the fallibility of the most carefully constituted tribunals. In 1865, for instance, an Italian named Pelizzioni was tried before Baron Martin for the murder of a fellow countryman in an affray at Saffron Hill. After an elaborate trial he was found guilty and sentenced to death. In passing sentence, the Judge took occasion to make the following remarks, which should be remembered when the acumen begotten of 'sound legal training' and long experience is relied on as a safeguard against error: 'In my judgment, it is utterly impossible for the jury to have come to any other conclusion. The evidence was about the clearest and most direct that, after a long course of experience in the administration of criminal justice, I have ever known. I am as satisfied as I can be of anything that Gregorio did not inflict this wound, and that you were the person who did.'

"The trial was over. The Home Secretary would most certainly, after the Judge's expression of opinion, never have interfered. The date of the execution was fixed. Yet the unhappy prisoner was guiltless of the crime, and it was only through the exertion of a private individual that an innocent man was saved from the gallows. A fellow countryman of his, a Mr. Negretti, succeeded in persuading the real culprit (the Gregorio so expressly exculpated by the Judge) to come forward and acknowledge the crime. He was subsequently tried for manslaughter and convicted, while Pellizioni received a free pardon.

"Again, in 1877, two men named Jackson and Greenwood were tried at the Liverpool Assizes for a serious offense. They were found guilty. The Judge expressed approval of the verdict and sentenced them to ten years' penal servitude. Subsequently fresh facts came to light and the men received a free pardon.

"Once more, in 1879, Hebron was tried for the murder of a policeman. He was found guilty and sentenced to death. An agitation for a reprieve immediately followed. The sentence was commuted to penal servitude for life. Three years after, the notorious Peace, just before his execution for the murder of Mr. Diason, confessed that he had committed the murder for which Hebron had been sentenced."

Mr. Charles Burleigh Galbraith, writing for Friend's Intelligencer for October 6, 1906, says: "Juries and Judges are still falliable." Maud Ballington Booth, writing under date of September, 1908, gives details to two interesting cases: "A man was sentenced to life imprisonment and served sixteen and a half years. Most of the evidence had been purely circumstantial and he was convicted mainly on the testimony of one witness. He was saved from the gallows only by the earnest efforts of those who had known of his previous good character. Last winter the woman who had been the main witness against him came to what she believed was her death bed, and, sending for a priest, confessed that she had committed perjury. The matter was brought to the attention of the Governor, and the man at once liberated. He still lives. The State took sixteen years of his liberty, but did not shed his innocent blood."

"At present I know a man," continues Mrs. Booth, "who has served nine years and is still in prison, where he has been visited by the boy whom he was supposed to have murdered.
"The fact that, in our day, justice may thus miscarry, must give men constant pause before they seek remedial vengeance in the death penalty."

Mr. Buttram, present Attorney-General for the Second Judicial District of Tennessee, in talking to me recently, said: "I am against capital punishment because men are too liable to err. Before I was elected Attorney-General, a white man was convicted in my county of murder in the first degree. He pleaded accidental killing. He was a poor fellow, and the Court had appointed a lawyer to defend him. I thought at the time the verdict was rendered that the jury had erred. The people were bitter against him and had threatened to lynch him. Some of the jury wanted to hang him outright, but they finally reported mitigating circumstances as a part of their verdict and the Judge sentenced the prisoner to life imprisonment. From later developments it became evident that the man was innocent, and for that reason Governor Hooper pardoned him recently.

Mr. Scruggs, former Secretary to ex-Governor Patterson, states on his honor that, while he was serving as said ex-Governor's Secretary, an innocent negro was hanged, as it developed subsequent to the hanging.

Mr. Duke C. Bowers had a cousin convicted on a charge of murder and sentenced to be hanged, but his sentence was commuted to life imprisonment by the Governor of Texas, through the intervention of the prisoner's wife. After serving twelve years, the man who had committed the murder for which the prisoner was sentenced confessed on his dying bed that he had committed said offense, and the prisoner was released.

From experience and observation, we know that many men who are innocent are convicted of various grades of crime, and that the greater the crime the more it arouses the passions of men, and the more apt to procure an unjust verdict through prejudice. Every lawyer knows how easy it is to convict the poor and friendless fellow charged with crime, and how hard to convict the man who has the influence and "pull." The present laws and practice foster extremes in both of said instances. Thus in the name of Justice, in order to vindicate a barbarous law, the State itself commits murder.

SOCIOLOGICAL REASON.

There is another reason, almost fundamental why society should not execute its befallen members. That reason is a sociological one. Experience shows that the great majority of criminals are either born criminals or their invironment promoted criminal instincts and even criminal traits. Had organized government done its duty towards him, he never would have been a criminal. An investigation of the penitentiaries shows that the majority are illiterate. Many of them have had no moral or religious training, and, of course, none of them are criminals from choice. They are "weak vessels," depraved degenerates, and, in many instances, monomaniacs. Yet they hollo, "Hang him."

It is estimated by sociologists who have scientifically studied the question that 90 per cent of the crimes would have been prevented had care, and prudence, and charity been exercised by the State and muinicpal governments. For example, the four gunmen of New York City sentenced to be hanged. They are victims of environment. They had been agents for gambling houses and houses of ill-fame, and divided their spoils with the officers of the law elected by the people of a great city. In that manner the agents of society educated them in crime, and yet the State says they must forfeit their blood to the State that trained them in vice. They had been trained in the underworld from infancy to commit crimes till they became callous and did not scruple in taking life.

No State has the right to kill men when it contributes to their downfall. It owes them the duty to educate them and throw nothing but moral influences around them, and when it fails, organized society is at fault. You may ask, "What will we do with them?"

Why, do your duty towards them, by placing them in a prison, reformatory in its character, and teach them morality, and, if necessary, give them mental training, and allow them the right to expirate their crimes and prepare for the hereafter. Make men out of them, and give them in the most, if not all instances, the hope that they will be rewarded if they will reform and become worthy of again taking their places among their fellowmen.

THE FALLACY IN THE PLEA FOR "RETRIBUTIVE JUSTICE."

But a few will say in this enlightened day even, that the criminal should be punished measure for measure for his crime. That is the old spirit of blood and vengeance that perished nearly two thousand years ago. That was a failure even under the old Jewish law, under which the penalty for every offense but one was death. Cain, Moses, Lamech, David, Simon and Levi were all murders, yet none were deprived of their lives on that account. Under that old law of revenge, the wife who believed in a different God from her husband forfeited her life, and slavery and polygamy were as much sanctioned by God as the law of murder, and yet no one would say it was not right to abolish them.

When Christ came and died for his enemies, he impliedly forbade us to kill our enemies. He forgave his murderers, saying, "Father, forgive them, for they know not what they do." Father Mathew says: "I have been in the ministry for thirty years, and I have never yet discovered that the founder of Christianity has delegated to any man any right to take away the life of his fellow-man." I did not intend going into that phase of the case, but refer you to the articles printed in the appendix hereto.

ABOLITION WOULD NOT INCREASE LYNCHING.

It is claimed by the advocates of the death penalty that if it is abrogated, it would increase lynching. Here again statistics come to our aid. In the State that have abolished the death penalty there has not been a lynching in several years, while there were eighteen men in the United States last year who were executed for rape, from January 1, 1912, to November 15, 1912; fifteen were lynched, leaving only three. We do not think conditions would be made worse.

A learned statesman and criminologist has said: "The death penalty as inflicted by governments is a perpetual excuse for mobs. The greatest danger in a republic is a mob, and as long as States inflict the penalty of death, mobs will follow the example. If the State does not consider life sacred, the mob, with ready rope, will strangle the suspected. The mob will say· "The only difference is the trial; we know he is guilty. Why should time be wasted in techincalities?"

In other words, why may not the mob do quickly what the law does slowly?

PARDONING LIFE PRISONERS.

Some members of the Legislature have said they would be for the bill if the Governor did not have the pardoning power. The records show that 89 per cent of those given a life sentence die in the penitentiary; that only 5 3-10 per cent are pardoned, and 5 7-10 are commuted, and not a single life prisoner has ever escaped from said prison. We know that a large per cent of the few who were pardoned were pardoned so they could die out of the prison walls, as was Lee Holder. Besides, when you assume they will be pardoned wrongfully, you assume you will elect corrupt Governors, which is ·not likely to occur.

Out of 150 life prisoners received at the State prison within the last ten years, only seven have been pardoned, some to die outside the walls, and one because it developed that he was innocent.

CONCLUSION.

I want to say that it is no "maudlin sentiment," nor misplaced sympathy, that moved the parties whom I represent to work for the passage of this measure. We have no interest except the best interest of the old "Volunteer State" and her hospitable citizenship.

For the foregoing reasons, we respectfully but earnestly request you, and each of you, to use your vote and influence for the passage of this bill.

Respectfully submitted,
R. L. SUDDATH, *Attorney,*
On Behalf of Himself, Duke C. Bowers, Et Als.

OPINIONS OF OTHERS.

The following opinions are taken from different periods of thought relative to this subject:

Andrew J. Palm: "It needs no extraordinary judgment to comprehend the truth that if government wishes to teach that life is sacred it must not set the example of deliberately destroying it. As well might it steal from the thief or burn the house of the incendiary as to snuff out a human life to teach that human life is sacred and should be held inviolable. The evil force of bad example is the strongest argument that can be made against the death penalty, and in itself should be sufficient to the law of life for life in every civilized country. ... The man who has a high regard for life needs no law to restrain his hand from murder."

Mr. B. Paul Neuman says: "Lord Ellenborough predicted chaos if men were not to be hanged for petit larceny, and Lord Eldon heartily agreed." .

G. Raleigh Vicars: "The obstacles in the way of determining the mental condition of a man makes hanging a dangerous and unjust method of punishment, and is a major objection to the same."

Lafayette: "I shall insist on having the death penalty abolished until I have the infallibility of human judgment demonstrated to me."

Elizabeth Cady Stanton: "You ask me if I believe in capital punishment. Indeed, I do not. When men are dangerous to the public they should be imprisoned; that done, the remaining consideration is the highest good of the prisoner. Crime is a disease; hence our prisons should be moral seminaries, where all that is true and noble in man should be nurtured into life. Our jails, our prisons, our whole idea of punishment is wrong, and will be until the mother soul is represented in our criminal legislation. It makes me shudder to think of the cruelties that are inflicted on criminals in the name of justice, and of the awful waste of life and force—of the crushing out of hundreds and thousands of noble men and promising boys in these abominable bastiles of the present country. "As to the gallows, it is the torture of my life. Every sentence and every execution I hear of is a break in the current of my life and thought today. I make my son the victim. I am with him in the solitude of that last awful night, broken only by the sound of the hammer and the coarse jeers of men, in preparation of the dismal pageant of the coming day. I see the cold sweat of death upon his brow, and weigh the mountains of sorrows that rest upon his soul, with its sad memories of the past, and fearful fore-bodings of the world to come. I imagine the mortal agony, the death struggle, and I know ten thousand mothers all over the land weep and pray and groan with me over every soul that is lost. Woman knows the cost of life better than man does.

'There will be no gallows, no dungeon, no heedless cruelty in solitiude when mothers make the laws."

William Cullen Bryant: "I am heartily with you, as you know, in your warfare against the barbarous practice of punishment by death, and my prayer is that your labor may be crowned with perfect success. Sooner or later I am confident that the infliction of the punishment of death by the law will become as obsolete to the civilized world as torture by the rack."

John G. Whittier: "I have given the subject of capital punishment much consideration, and have no hesitation in saying that I do not regard the death penalty essential to the security and well-being of society; on the contrary, I believe that its total abolition, and the greater certainty of conviction which would follow, would tend to diminish rather than increase the crimes it is intended to prevent."

Alice Carey: "I cannot, probably, add anything to the force of what must have been already said by your contributors against the crime of crimes—capital punishment. As I regard it, the second murder is worse than the first; for the first may have been attended with extenuating circumstances—not so the second."

Henry W. Longfellow: "I am, and have been for many years, an opponent of capital punishment. It would be useless to state my reasons. They are, in the main, the same, doubtless, as those which influence the other opponents to the death penalty."

Horatio Seymour: "I do not know exactly how far we shall agree with regard to capital punishment. I am decidedly in favor of softening our criminal code for many reasons. By so doing we shall secure greater certainty of conviction in cases of guilt. I am a strong believer in the influence of hope, rather than fear. The longer I live and the more I see and learn of men, the more I am disposed to think well of their hearts and poorly of their heads."

Dr. Benjamin Rush: "The power over human life is the sole prerogative of him who gave it. Human laws, therefore, are in rebellion against this prerogative when they transmit it to human hands. I have said nothing of the punishment of death for murder, because I consider it an improper punishment for any offense."

Father Matthew: "I have been about thirty years in the ministry and I have never yet discovered that the founder of Chris tianity has delegated to man any right to take away the life of his fellowman."

Henry Ward Beecher: "In our age, and with the resources which Christian civilization has placed within reach of civil governments, there is no need of the death penalty, and every consideration of reason and humanity pleads for its abolition. It does not answer well the ends of justice, and often defeats them. As an example, it tends rather to brutify than to quicken the moral sense of spectators, and yet, while the fear of hanging does not deter men from crime, the fear of inflicting death deters many a jury from finding a just verdict and favors the escape of criminals. It is the rude justice of a barbarous age. We ought, long ago, to have done with it."

Wendell Phillips: "The gallows should be abolished altogether. It never could have been defended, except on the ground of absolute necessity, in order to protect society. It would be absurd to make any such plea for it now, since we all know that, within the resources of modern times, we can keep a man within four walls as long as we see fit. That guards the community, and we have no right to punish him in order to deter others from following in his footsteps. The moment a man violates law he forfeits his civil right. This gives society the right, and it imposes on it the duty, of subjecting hm to the best moral nfluences it can command, as long as it needs to make him a good citizen. That is all the right society acquires over him, and this does not justify the gallows."

Victor Hugo: "The law that dips its finger in human blood to write the commandment, 'Thou shalt not murder,' is naught but an example of legal transgression against the precept itself."

Robert Burns: "Man's inhumanity to man makes countless thousands mourn."

William Shakespeare:

> "The jury, passing on the prisoner's life,
> May, in the sworn twelve, have a thief or two
> Guiltier than him they try."

Cicero: "Away with the executioner and the execution, and the very name of its engine. Even the mere mention of them is unworthy of a Roman citizen and a freeamn."

Francis Bacon: "There is no passion in the mind of man so weak that it mates and masters the fear of death. Revenge triumphs over death, love slights it, honor aspireth to it, and grief fleeth to it."

Arthur C. Mellette, a former Governor of South Dakota, has this to say of capital punishment: "I have long been of the opinion that capital punishment fosters crime and murder, and that imprisonment for life, without power of pardon, would better subserve the interest of society."

Former Justice of the United States Supreme Court Samuel F. Miller, on the day before his death, wrote as follows: "I have only to say that I am now, and have been for many years, a disbeliever in the merits of capital punishment as a means of preventing crime. A long judicial experience has impressed me more and more with the force of the argument against the policy of such punishment, but I have not abandoned my original belief against the moral right of taking life as a judicial proceeding.

"You would, perhaps, be interested to know that the following sentence is a part of a judgment delivered by me in the Circuit Court of the United States for the District of Iowa, 1867, and is to be found in the case of United States vs. Gleason, Woolworth Reports, 140:

" 'The penalty which the law attaches to your offense is one which my private judgment does not approve, for I do not believe that capital punishment is the best means to enforce the observance of the laws, or that, in the present state of society, it is necessary for its protection, but I have no more right, for that reason, to refuse to obey the law than you have to resist it.'"

CAPITAL PUNISHMENT.

By W. T. Bolling, *D.D.*

Has man any moral right to take the life of his fellow-man, under any circumstances, except to save his own life? I think not, because the divine law says: "Thou shalt not kill, and when God says this He either means it, or indulges in grim humor, which would destroy the confidence of man in the sincerity of the Great Lawmaker, and practically would destroy the entire decalogue as of binding force, and excuse all crime. '

If God made provision to depart from this commandment, He provided for the abrogation of every commandment under certain conditions. "Thou shalt not steal" would mean that thou shalt not illegally steal, but may steal when the human law provides for it. So might we deal with every commandment and nullify all of them. I take it for granted that God meant what He said when He gave the moral code to Moses at Sinai, and if so, man has no right to amend the divinely made and given law, and therefore has no right to take the life of his fellow-man. under any condition, unless it be to preserve his own life, and prevent its being taken by another.

No man or body of men cant justly claim the right to take what he or they cannot restore, and because human-made law provides for conditions under which man may take the life of man, in no wise alters the moral crime involved in doing so.

It is urged that capital punishment is necessary in order to maintain government, but this is a mere assumption without proof, for government in States and counties which have abandoned capital punishment is as good, if not better, than in those States which still use this mode of punishment. To take a man's life is no punishment, so far as this life is concerned, and man has no power to punish in the world to come. Really punishment is only in relation to this life so far as man can inflict or suffer it, and to claim that the State takes the life of a man to punish him is sheer folly. Life imprisonment would be real punishment, and with man living and yet alone in self-communion, and in the presence of his crime and folly, would far surpass death as a punishment for the taking of the life of his fellow-man.

Many a man, under the burden of his sin and shame, has taken his own life, because death is far preferable to being compelled to live in presence of conscious crime and remorse for having committed it. True, many a man has petitioned for the commuting of the death sentence to life imprisonment, but in nine cases out of ten it is done under the hope of pardon; and take away this hope, and the same men would prefer death to life imprisonment, for then death would be the least of the two punishments.

The taking of criminal life is but a relic of heathenism, and utterly antagonistic to the law of God and Christian civilization. It does not bring back the dead; and, in humanity, satisfies only the low spirit of revenge in the living—a spirit murderously criminal within itself, and severely rebuked by the Christ himself. "Ye have heard it said, in olden times, an eye for an eye, and a tooth for a tooth, but I say unto you, love your enemies, and pray for them that dispitefully use you," and the taking of human life is out of harmony with this teaching.

Imprisonment for life gives the criminal some opportunity for reformation, and at the same time puts the seal of contamination upon his crime beyond any that can be put by depriving him of life. Add to this the withdrawal of the power of pardon from the Governor, making a life sentence be for life, unless it can be shown that an innocent man has been wrongfully condemned, and this through a board of pardons, and then we would have punishment for the guilty and vindication for the innocent, meeting the design of all just law, which is not for taking revenge upon the guilty, but to punish the guilty in order to protect society and to vindicate the innocent. Since the individual nor the State cannot give life, neither has any right to take it, as that right is alone lodged in the Great Giver of all Life, and the province of the State is to deal with the living along the lines of life, punishing for the present only, with no power to deal with

the things and conditions of the future life. What adequate satisfaction to the individual or the State can there be in the taking of a human life, unless it be to satisfy a spirit of revenge, which has no place in the divine law, and should have none in human law. To imprison for life, depriving man of his liberty and all citizen privileges, while at the same time protecting society, is reasonable, just and even humane, and beyond this is but a usurpation of power upon the part of the State in the exercise of the power of life or death, which alone belongs to God.

If we are to judge by the past, the taking of human life by the State is no remedy for crime, for in the face of possible death murder is alarmingly on the increase, and human life was never so cheap as it is at present, and certainly there is a demand for some other deterring preventive of crime, for capital punishment is a failure. With capital punishment the penalty for crime, it is difficult to get a jury to convict, because the taking of human life is repugnant to even the coarsest type of mankind, and utterly out of all harmony with refined nature, so that even unconsciously men recoil from the idea of taking human life—men who would readily give a verdict for life imprisonment compromise on acquittal.

Of course, I am aware that many will disagree with me, for I have never been able to get everybody to see my way and be right in their view, but I am sure that, as men grow more civilized, capital punishment grows less popular and wholesale murder, in the shape of war, is regarded as the last resort by the civilized nations of earth, and the time will come when human life will be rightly valued and war shall be no more.

If this is not to be the case Christianity will have proved a failure, to become an effete religion, cast by intelligent humanity upon the religious scrap-pile of the ages.

Is it not time to put aside the unwarranted penalty of capital punishment and adopt the more humane and effective punishment by life imprisonment, put beyond the reach of one-man pardon?

The capital punishment experiment has proved a failure, so far as it being a remedy for crime is concerned, and we certainly should cease to officially commit the crime for which we hang the other fellow.—*Memphis Commercial Appeal*, January 26, 1913.

DETECTIVE AGAINST IT.

Stout Says Capital Punishment Should Be Abolished.

"Capital punishment does not act as any benefit in deterring crime," said J. T. Stout, Chief of the Stout Detective Agency, talking with a reporter for The Democrat yesterday.

"I think that the principle of taking a life for a life is entirely wrong, and should be abolished. My long experience as a detective has shown me that it does not carry out the fullest aims of justice.

"We have capital punishment in this State today and yet crime still continues, especially murder. I believe in giving every man a chance if possible, and I think that imprisonment for life would at least give a man a chance to lead a decent life in prison, where otherwise he would be dead. Then if in prison he is of that much value to the State as a laborer, whereas dead men can't work."—*Nashville Democrat*.

By H. W. Lewis.

There are many persons who do not want to investigate progressive ideas in the treatment of crime and criminals, those who believe in blood for blood, and who do not want to believe anything else can find the sum total of the argument in its favor in the Pentateuch.

An ignorant conscience is an uncertain guide. Slavery was an institution of so long standing that it was assented to as right and proper without investigation on the part of the great majority. Arguments in favor of slavery were drawn from the Scriptures, and it was defended from the pulpit as a divine institution because Moses held it to be such. Many persons are displeased with the idea of doing away with the death penalty, and charge the origin of such ideas as a disbelief in the Sacred Word. These people have a strong sentiment for the Bible, but it is mostly a mere sentiment. The two verses, "Whoso sheddeth man's blood by man shall his blood be shed," and the one like unto it, "He that spareth the rod hateth his son," constitute the sum total of their knowledge of the Old Testament, while their respect for the new is based largely on Paul's advice to Timothy, to take a little wine for his stomach's sake. They are just as firm in the faith of hanging, whipping and moderate drinking as if they had much more authority for their position. Many persons, usually in the rear of the van of progress, want "Thus saith the Lord" for everything they undertake, and while waiting for the "still small voice" to come with sufficient force to set them in action, others grasp the situation, go ahead, on the principle that the Lord helps those that help themselves, set the wheels of reform in motion, and these obstructionists come up just in time to say "amen" and thank the Lord that the victory was won by faith and prayer.

It will not be denied that slavery was defended from the pulpit less than seventy years ago, North and South.

The tendency on the part of the clergy to be conservative may be accounted for on the ground that they draw their inspiration, and the principles by which they are governed, largely from what has been aptly called the "carpenter" theory of creation. They make no allowances for the race to grow, but think that what was good enough for Abraham and Moses four or five thousand years ago is good enough for Tennesseans in this, the twentieth century.

It is hardly necessary to add that ministers, as a body, are ardent advocates of the law that demands blood for blood, and they can justly claim the credit, whatever it may be, for having kept the old law so long in force. Some of their ablest men, however, who, by the way, are usually the most liberal, are opposed to overcoming evil with evil, and have had the courage so to express themselves.

When ministers become convinced that it is their duty to fight a custom they go into the contest in earnest. As soon as the preachers were satisfied that slavery in Judea did not make slavery right in Tennessee, they went at it "tooth and nail," and did much to create the impression that banished slavery from existence. If the time comes when they outgrow another Jewish custom, when they believe what they preach—that the vilest sinner may return, that forgiveness, mercy, and amity are better. than vengeance, retaliation, and blood—then death as a punishment for crime will be relegated to its proper place among the relics of a lower degree of civilization. Suppose we found our criminal jurisprudence on the Mosaic code, what crimes or offenses would be punishable with death? Here is a list that includes many of them: Murder, kidnaping, eating leavened bread during the Passover, allowing a cross ox to kill a person, witchcraft, bestiality, idolatry, oppression of widows and orphans, making holy ointment, violation of the Sabbath, striking father or mother, sodomy, eating the flesh of the peace offering with uncleanliness, eating any manner of blood, offering children to Moloch, screening an idolator, going after familiar spirits, unchastity before marriage, when charged by the husband or unchastity of a priest's daughter, blasphemy, forbearing to keep the Passover, uncleanliness, stranger coming near the tabernacle, and a number of others.

No matter how great any man's respect for the Old Tatament may be, the most that he can say for the ceremonial and criminal law of the Hebrews is that it was adapted to men in a very crude condition, who were making their first advances in the rudiments of moral and religious truths; that it taught them only as much as they were prepared to receive, with a promise of something better to come after. Ministers admit that the ceremonial law of the Jews is no longer binding, and that the criminal code has no force except in case of numbers. They insist that God's covenant with Noah, in which occurs the verse. "Whoso sheddeth man's blood by man shall his blood be shed," is binding for all time and upon all nations. They do not understand that it is repealed, both in the language and the spirit of the New Testament. If they believe as firmly as they pretend that killing the murderer is pleasing to God and a duty sacredly enjoined upon man, they should act as executioners: they certainly should not hesitate to pull the string or cut the rope that sends the soul of a murderer to the answering bar of God.

The prinicples of the Jewish law of penal jurisprudence are so diametrically opposed to the spirit of Christianity that there can be no compromise between them. Either Christ's command when He says, "Ye have heard that it hath been said an eye for an eye, and a tooth for a tooth, but I say unto you, that ye resist not evil," must prevail, or the very thing He forbids must be ac knowledged as right. Moses put his enemies to death, Christ died for them; Moses was sinful, Christ was sinless; Moses insisted on sacrifice, Christ required mercy; Moses was a lawgiver and teacher for a single nation, Christ gave a gospel for the world."

If Jesus had not given His thought on this law of Moses, as found in the Sermon on the Mount; if he had not set up a standard immeasurably higher, then we might pretend that this law of Moses for the punishment of murder was a statement for all generations and all forms of civilization. But His teaching is actually as much or more in advance of Moses' law as that was in advance of the ideas and practices of men when it was given. But this law of Moses is all there is in the Bible which can be pleaded as an exception to the commandment, "Thou shalt not kill." Jesus did enforce this law against killing, but He did not, directly or indirectly, recognize any exception to it. "Thou shalt not kill" is more a command than God's covenant with Noah. It is binding on nations as well as on individuals, for there are no exceptions provided. What right have we to make any?—*Nashville Banner.*

THE FEAR OF DEATH.

Government statistics show an average of 1,600 homicides committed per year, for the past ten years, in the United States and 5,500 suicides per year during the same time.

Which conclusively proves that the fear of death does not deter when desperation takes hold of a man.

Putting people to death did not deter the Christian religion, but, on the other hand, made it the most powerful religion in the world.

Christ, who was put to death by a howling mob, and who had the power to save himself, exemplified and proved the correct. ness of the doctrine which He preached. "Vengeance is mine, saith the Lord." "Be not overcome with evil, but overcome evil with good."—*Duke C. Bowers.*

BOWERS, OPPOSER OF DEATH PENALTY, MAKING HARD FIGHT.

Duke C. Bowers, retired grocery merchant of Memphis, has returned to Nashville to resume his fight for the passage of a bill in the Legislature abolishing capital punishment in Tennessee. Mr. Bowers is entering into the fight with great enthusiasm, and is making a telling campaign among the legislators and with the public. Largely through his efforts the issue of capital punishment has been brought before the people of Tennessee, and will be kept before them until after the bill in the Legislature is passed or defeated.

Mr. Bowers has made the abolition of capital punishment his study for many years, and is thoroughly familiar with the subject. The following interview was given out by him Monday night:

"Capital punishment has been abolished in five States. In each of these States, with one exception, homicides have been on the decrease, while in the neighboring States, in almost every instance, homicides are on the increase.

"The government reports regarding the States on which tab is kept as to homicides and so forth showed that, taking the whole as an average, there are almost two and one-half times as many homicides in those States that have the death penalty as against those that have done away with it.

Mob Law Argument.

"Some argue that mob law will increase if the death penalty is abolished. Statistics show that from June 1, 1912, to November 15, 1912, there were eighteen people killed in the United States for rape, of which number fifteen were lynched and three were executed, which refutes the above argument, because fifteen out of eighteen are already being lynched.

"Others argue that so long as the pardon power remains with the Governor that they are against the abolishing of the death penalty. There have been received at the Nashville penitentiary in the past ten years 151 life-time prisoners, and during that time only seven have been pardoned. Some of them having been so as to let them die at home with their people, one of them because the jury and court that tried the man decided he was not guilty, and anyone with a heart in him would have done what the Governors did in these cases.

"The old doctrine of 'an eye for an eye' was done away with by that Great Teacher who said, 'Be not overcome of evil, but overcome evil with good.' 'Vengeance is mine, saith the Lord.'

FEAR OF DEATH.

"The fear of death does not deter homicides. For the past ten years there have been an average of about 1,600 homicides and 5,500 suicides per year, showing that when desperation takes hold of a man the fear of death does not deter him from taking even his own life. The fear of death did not prevent our ancestors from joining the army in defense of our country. If the fear of death had prevailed, then our State would not bear the name of the Volunteer State.

"The death penalty is ghastly, inhuman, unchristlike, barbarous and absolutely inexcusable from statistical standpoints as well as from all other standpoints.

"Part of the taxes you pay, I pay, and all of us pay, is being paid someone in this State for the purpose of having him take some poor, weak, misguided, unfortunate human being out and hang him by the neck until he is dead, dead, dead.

"Who is able to know that we would not have committed the same crime for which this God-given human soul was put to death, had we have sprung from the same ancestry, been thrown in the same environment and have been cursed with the same devils? Who knows but what in the sight of God we commit as great a wrong when we take His name in vain as does the vilest lawbreaker in his misdeeds?

"Help us to be merciful unto others as we would have God be merciful unto us."—*Nashville Tennessean and American.*

DR. PAYNE AGAINST CAPITAL PUNISHMENT.

Educator Declares Barbarous Custom Does Not Act as Crime Deterrent.

"All of my feelings are against capital punishment, and always have been," said Dr. Bruce R. Payne, President of the George Peabody College, talking with a reporter for The Democrat last night.

"Even the thought of capital punishment is cruel, and I think that such method of punishment is unnecessary. It is rather a barbarous custom, and theoretically does not reach its ends.

"When a State punishes a criminal and at the same time repairs a broken life, I think it is far better than snuffing life out, thereby neither helping in reformation nor deterring crime."

When asked if he thought the bill introduced yesterday was a good one, and should be passed, Dr. Payne replied:

"Well, yes, it is a good thing, and should be passed. Capital punishment doesn't seem to get anywhere, so to speak. If a criminal is dangerous to society, then lock him up.

"Frequently the very lowest type of criminals represented in the South by the negroes considers it not dishonorable, but rather distinguishing, for members of his class to die the ostentatious death on the scaffold.

"On the other hand, the example of long years of imprisonment, or enforced labor on pubilc works proves a much stronger deterring influence than capital punishment."—*The Democrat.*

DR. PARRISH AGAINST CAPITAL PUNISHMENT.

"I am totally against capital punishment in any form," said Dr. H. B. Parrish, one of Nashville's prominent physicians, and the Councilman from the Twentieth Ward, talking with a reporter for The Democrat. "And I am willing to do anything in reason to do away with it.

"Capital punishment is barbarous, and inhuman, and anything but the right thing. I do not think that it is the correct thing for a civilized community to have such a law on its statute books.

"No man has a right to take something which he cannot restore, as I see it, and therefore the State has no right to take the life of a man which it cannot give back.

"I think that the bill introduced by Charles C. Gilbert and others in the Legislature is an excellent one, and I certainly hope that it will go through.

"From the standpoint of humanity, civilization and Christianity, we should do away with capital punishment."—*The Democrat*.

POPULAR PASTOR AGAINST LEGAL KILLING.

"I prefer to learn towards mercy's side," said Dr. Carey E. Morgan, one of the most popular ministers in the city, and pastor of the Vine Street Christian Church, when asked last night if he was for the abolishment of capital punishment.

"My whole nature rebels against it, and, really, I'm with you for the abolishment. It does seem to me that, under the influence of Christianity, there should be some method of reformation as well as punishment.

"We are not under the ancient Mosaic law of 'an eye for an eye, and a tooth for a tooth,' but under the gospel of the grace of God. We are taught to 'love our enemies and do good to them that despitefully use us.'

"It seem that some method looking toward the reformation rather than the sheer punishment would be more Christian, and, perhaps, finally would serve as a surer protection for society."
—*The Democrat*.

PROMINENT RECTOR OPPOSES DEATH PENALTY.

"I am heartily opposed to capital punishment," said Rev. Nicholas Rightor, assistant rector of St. Ann's Episcopal Church, when interviewed.

"I have always been against capital punishment, for I think that civilization and humanity demands reformation rather than punishment from a criminal, and when a man's life is napped out there is no opportunity for reformation, as far as the outer world is concerned.

"Capital punishment is a barbarous custom, for in this day and age we are not under the ancient law of Mosaic days, calling for an 'eye for an eye, and a tooth for a tooth.'—*The Democrat.*

"I have never been in favor of this method of punishing a criminal or making it an example for society, and I think it would be a good thing to abolish it.

"In this christian dispensation it is not for any man to usher another into the other life before his time."—*The Democrat.*

CRIME AND PUNISHMENT.

To the Editor of The Democrat:

Of real crime, all crimnologists affirm: First, that it is a social disease like insanity, of which it is really a form; and, second, that it is the result or effect of definite causes, and is not effected in the slightest degree by the infliction of punishment upon the criminal.

Government deals with this matter in a blundering, unscientific manner, the basis of which is the stupid and savage idea of revenge, the idea that crime is to be restrained, if not prevented, by examples of punishment.

Those who have made this problem a study very generally agree that punishment not only does not prevent or lessen crime, but tends, rather, to propagate it. This is so well understood taday that the death penalty is no longer made a public exhibition because of its demoralizing effects.

In those districts where the death penalty has been abolished no one is less safe than elsewhere. Since crime is a social disease, its cure or prevention can only be effected by the removal of the generating causes. The chief cause of crime is unnatural social conditions, such as poverty on the one hand and opulence on the other. Wealh, with its idleness, creates vice, for vicious living is characteristic of all aristocratic classes whose members are not obliged to labor and are compelled to find some way to amuse themselves in order to prevent ennui. Poverty, with its enforced idleness, tends also to dissipation and vicious propensities.

In a social system where neither of these extremes of poverty and wealth exists, and in which all are employed in some form of rational and useful activity, the incentive to vicious living will no longer exist, and vice and crime will naturally vanish for want of conditions to produce them. The establishment of rational social conditions will thus in time eliminate all crime, which is unnatural and would not exist under perfectly natural conditions.

ELVIRO D. LAURA.

Nashville, February 2.

THE TREND OF CAPITAI PUNISHMENT.

Editor Tennessean and American:

The taking of life in punishment for offenses against society is as old as the human race. It is very natural the idea of such punishment would suggest itself to primitive and barbarous people. To put the offender out of existence was the first way thought of. Thus we find in both sacred and profane history the death penalty inflicted for countless offenses. In dark days we find it caused very little disgust even to the most sensitive natures.

Early writers speak lightly of it. What is ghastly impression is made when we find Ovid, at a time when the sexes were seated together at Rome to witness the executions of criminals, speaking of this as a "fit place for a lover to prosecute his suit l" Increased intensity of seriousness may be observed with the growth of literature. Strange that Nero, "the monster of cruelty," should say during the first few years of his reign, when death warrants were presented him to sign, that he regretted he had ever learned to write, so averse was he to shedding human blood. Later, when he became brutalized, he could sign them without pain, and put his own mother to death without remorse. In the middle ages the church, the Christian church, put to death thousands who refused to accept its theological dogmas.

In the reign of George III of England, only a century and a half ago, above 300 offenses were capital. Goldsmith and his disciples began to recast the public conscience. A few years later Sir Samuel Romilly, slavery and law reformer, fought vigorously for abolition of the death penalty. Humane societies played their part. One crime after another has been stricken from the list till only two are left—high treason and first degree murder. In 1864 the question of complete abolition was considered by a royal commission. They reported two years later differing on expediency, and recommending that it be confined to first degree murder. English juries now seldom give a first degree verdict, and when they do, the sentence is not often carried out, for the crown reserves the right to change sentence, and frequently does.

In continental Europe, perhaps Beccaria, philanthropic writer of the eighteenth century, was foremost in diminishing capital punishment. Norway, Roumania, Portugal, Holland, and fifteen of the twenty-two cantons of Switzerland, have completely abolished it, while the larger countries have reduced capital offenses to a few. In France, when death sentence is pronounced, mercy is greatly exercised by the president.

In our own country four states—Maine, Michigan, Wisconsin and Rhode Island—no longer inflict the death penalty. The capital offenses of the states retaining it vary from one to four. Others have considered, and are still considering, abolition. In Virginia's last general assembly the subject received no little attention. Recently in Oregon we find Governor West urging the people to abolish it by vote.

Next, the methods of infliction. Naturally, when the death penalty would suggest itself to the race in its infancy, the most cruel and torturing means would be thought of. The trend is significant—burning, crucifixion, impalement, precipitation from rocks, stoning, beheading, poisoning, hanging, electric shock. In early ages executions were public, the community taking part. Today only the morbidly curious or the brutally disposed would care to witness an execution. Only a few would hold that a public execution frightens the criminally inclined. Second to a free lynching in demoralizing a community is a free execution. Hence most Christian countries debar the public. Hence secular newspapers that are inclined to swell their columns with gruesome details to gratify the morbidly curious are debarred. Such is a very meagre account of the subject. It is significant. Commenting is in order.

Who do people sanction capital punishment when it is so generally accepted as a relic of barbarism that it has become a truism?

First, it is an ingrained habit. It is a case of persistent racial habit developing almost into an instinct.

Secondly, lawmakers do not err. A good citizen will honor and respect the sacred charge of a legislative body. A citizen is not necessarily bad if he does not agree with every expression. They sometimes hold that the licensed saloon is for the best interest of the State. Many are not persuaded.

Thirdly, some accept every expression as they do Chicago canned labeled goods. They swallow and think no more.

Fourthly, the brutality of crime justifies it. Yes, some crimes are brutal—brutal beyond conception of the ordinary mind. But to balance brutality and play the part of a savage is unworthy of a great and humane people.

Fifthly, it is a great deterrent of crime. If so, records of the foreign countries, the States in our own country that have abolished it ,and the personal testimony of Governors and officials are meaningless. Some States and nations have abolished and restored. It is noteworthy that in the majority of such instances no difference in rate of crime could be observed.

Sixthly, Scripture justifies it. With all reverence, passages can be transposed literally to fit either side, strained and distorted to carry points. Most of the passages justifying it are found in the shady portions of the history of the race. We do not expect for men to see as well at mifnight as at noonday. I cannot harmonize the taking of human life for offenses with the heart of Christ.

Seventhly, the law gives ample time for a condemned person to prepare for eternity. If there is a future existence of the soul, what person can say, what person would dare say, when a soul is ready to meet its God? We do not live by the click of a clock. Preparation for eternity is not a mechanical process having a common measure. A pliant heart may prepare in a brief period. An obdurate heart may require years. Surely the person who commits a capital offense is most likely to be the latter. Hence the power to settle a person's fate irrevocably can be exercised justly only by the Omniscient.

Personally, were I to take the life of the vilest human being conceivable. I should be guilty of his blood. And according to Christ's teachings to sanction the same by others I must be equally as guilty. Pardon the sentiment, but if my life were taken by another, I should only want my avengers to confine my slayer in some place where the light from heaven could serve to transform him more into the likeness of his Maker.

Above is the trend; following, the comment. I believe, with many others, I can repeat, feeling innocent of maudlin sentiment, or of being an enemy of the common weal, the closing lines of Myra Townsend's poem on the subject

"Cease not from striving, till our law
    Is clear from bloody stain,
And reformation—not revenge—
    In principle sustain."

                        L. W. HENDRICKSON.

Nashville, Tenn.

CAPITAL PUNISHMENT IS MURDER!

The following news item from Special Correspondent W. G. Shepherd appeared in The Memphis Press, February 17, 1912. Read it:

CHICAGO, February 17.—"How did my boy die?"

It wasn't a mother or a father asking a question. It was a deputy sheriff, who stood on the gallows looking down at the swinging form of an 18-year-old boy about whose neck he had fastened a rope five minutes before.

"Wasn't his neck broken?" insisted the deputy, talking to one of the dozen doctors who were examining the boy's body. When the doctor answered in the affirmative the deputy stepped back from the trap-hole, satisfied.

What you see at a hanging is one thing: it shows you what society is doing to criminals. But what you hear at hangings shows you what society is doing to itself when it takes the life of a human being.

I'm going to put down what I heard—the talk of men—at the hanging of Phillip Summerling, 34 years; Thos. Schultz, 18 years; Ewald Shiblawaski, 24; Ewald's brother, Frank, 21, and Thos. Jennings, negro, 35.

For two hours and ten minutes there were gathered in the

vast, high-ceilinged room forty-five physicians, thirty-five guards and twenty newspaper men. They were the representatives of society, and I want to show by the things I heard them say what hanging does to the men who are not hanged.

In his office, before we went into the death chamber, I asked Deputy Sheriff Peters how many men he had hung.

"Why, young fellow," he said, "I hung men before you were born. I hung the Haymarket rioters. And I've hung forty men," he added proudly.

"Have a smoke," some one said to Peters.

"No. No smokes, eats or drinks until this job is done. Then I'll go out and take a stiff drink of whisky. I always have a reaction after a hanging. It always makes me tired and sick."

"Doctors! Doctors!" exclaimed some one in the hallway.

We looked out of Peter's office and saw a double line of deputy sheriffs, leading from the main door of the jail. Between then was passing a line of forty-two physicians, who were being admitted to the death chamber.

Peters went to the telephone and called up the State's Attorney.

"There's a fellow who's trying a four-flush in Judge Landis' court to make us put off this hanging. It's a piece of hocus pocus.. The fellow just wants to get into the limelight. I want you to understand that I am going right along with this busi ness."

When he had hung up the receiver, Peters said to the deputy:

Fix up the sawbones! Get them in their chairs, and then we'll get busy."

"Press! Press!' 'a deputy called. That meant that the dozen newpaper men were to go into the death chamber.

A doctor tried to squeeze in with us.

"No, no; you can't go with these fellows. Sit down with the doctors. You can examine the corpse with them."

doctors all sat in chairs, at the foot of the high scaffolThe

I heard one doctor with whiskers talking to another.

"Hanging is all damn foolishness," he said. "Now here are

four good strong men. One of them has a penniless wife and baby. The murdered man left a penniless wife and baby. Why don't they put these four men in jail somewhere for life, and make them work to support the two penniless women and their babies? Ain't it damn foolishness to kill them?"

"I heard the guard say:
"There's a fellow in New York City who's the best executioner in the country. He's killed 140, and he never makes a miscue. Must have nerve, huh?"

"What'll you have to eat?" one reporter asked another when they sat down at a reporters' table that was covered with a white cloth.

"Yow! yow! pow! pow!" These noises came from the cell. Inmates of the jail were rattling their bars, yelling and pounding tin cups. The death march had begun.

"They'll show up around that corner in a minute," said one reporter. "I'm an old hand in this hanging room. I've seen 17 hangings here." There was a shuffle of feet on the iron floor and the procession walked onto the gallery from an upper tier. There was a priest, in white, officers in blue, and two men roughly drssed—the Shiblawski brothers.

All you could hear was the murmur of the priest's prayer and the murmur of the men, who repeated his words in low tones. What were they saying? What kind of a prayer do men make on a gollows?

No one could hear their words. The brothers kissed the cross which the priest held to them. While this was going on their legs and arms were being strapped. We tried to hear what they were saying as the deputies put a white shroud about their bodies, but we stopped trying when the white caps were tied over their heads. Everybody seemed to be working slowly on the gollows. One brother turned his muffled head toward another. We heard the murmur of his voice.

"Crash!" that was the next sound. Then came the scuffling of the feet of 14 doctors, as they walked to the two bags, their contents twitching, which hung from the swaying ropes.

The reporters rushed to a back room, where their telephone and telegraph wires had been placed. I caught these bits of news as they talked: "Just as the writhing body of the boy stopped swaying." "Strangled. gurgled." "Twitched like cats in a bag." "Oh, is that you taking my stuff, Bill? Great show! Great show. Three more to come."

"What, in Christmas, was that prayer?" said one reporter. "I don't know. Tell your office to look it up in the prayer book. They can copy it from that."

Two men were fixing up two other ropes. They carried out two bodies on a wheeled table. covered with a white cloth.

"Both of their necks were broken." said a doctor, coming to the reporters' table.

During the lull I talked to seven of the 14 doctors who had examined. I wanted to know whether they believed in capital punishment. Not a one of them did.

"Capital punishment doesn't keep people from committing murder, unless you hang men on a high gallows, in a big space. where all the folks in the city can see it," said Dr. A. C. Koethe.

'This is my first hanging, and my last," said Dr. I. E. Huffman. "After this I don't believe in capital punishment. I can see a patient die, but to see sane men kill a well man, in cold blood—excuse me."

All of this talk was sort of "between the acts."

"Hats off! No smoking," called a man in overalls, from the gallows.

The next sound was that of the prison inmates, who were watching the death watch. Then we heard the shuffle of feet, and again the priest and the deputies in blue brought two poorly dressed men onto the scaffold.

"Well, the other two got across in time for lunch, said one deputy in a seat near me, looking at his watch.

"These fellows'll eat with them," answered another guard. "But I guess they'll all get there too soon to please them."

The two men in poor clothes stood on the trap where the deputies placed them. One of them wasn't a man. but a boy, John Schultz, 18 years old, son of immigrants, who, as one reported said, "hadn't done anything but get into bad company." And now we know what the prayer was. for John raised his head and looked up, he fixed his blue eyes on the high ceiling, he repeated the words which the priest murmured.

"Oh, Christ: have mercy on my soul!" His words rang out, clear and distinct as a bell. "Holy Mary, intercede for me! Pray for me! Bring me to everlasting life."

The deputies were tying the straps about his arms and legs. Another of them tied the white shroud about the boy's neck. "Savior, save me. Forgive me my sins!"

"Listen to that young fellow pray," said a reporter.

"Christ, I love Thee!" said the boy. In the white covering he looked like a choir boy.

"Grant me to live wtih Thee. Forgive me my sins."

While he said these words, still looking upward, William Davies, the jailer, put the noose over his head and tightened the knot under the boy's ear.

Another deputy was doing the same thing to Simmerling.

"Forgive me my sins! Forgive me my sins!" rang out the voice of the boy. His voice was growing louder; there was a tone of wildness in it.

"Holy Mary!"—"Crash!" It was an awful thing to hear in the same moment those words from the mouth of that boy, and that sound. But they came together. Again the feet of fourteen doctors scuffled over the cement floor to the white, swaying, twitching bags.

There was another intermission.

"Now, if this nigger'll only confess before he's hung, you fellow'll get a fine top-off for your day's story," said a deputy sheriff to the reporters.

"We've got a good early start in the day's work," said a reporter. "Are you going out for lunch? Why don't you sheriffs go out now and then come back for the afternoon's work? You can finish a lot of men at this raet."

"Gee," said a young doctor, coming up to Jailer Davies. "I thought you'd left your handcuffs on that young fellow. I lifted up his hand, and I didn't see that another doctor was holding it by the elbow. I thought his hands were locked together, because I couldn't move his arms."

"They don't suffer," another doctor was telling the reporters.

"But isn't there some easier way to kill a man?" asked a reporter.

"I should say so," said the doctor. "They could put a tiny drop of hydrocyanic acid in his soup some day, and in an instant he would be stone dead, without a twitch or a pain. Or they could kill a man with morphine, and he would die pleasantly, in beautiful dreams. But this hanging! It's the crudest thing in civilization!"

"I saw a young doctor put young Schultz's neck back into place in fine shape," said a deputy—"just grabbed his head, gave it a twist and it snapped right back where it belonged."

I saw plenty of smiles during the two hours and ten minutes. I heard plenty of attempted jokes and commonplaces, among the 12 doctors and the reporters and deputies. Why did we smile and try to talk of everyday things?

Because hanging is so awful that a man who witnesses it dare not admit to himself how awful it is. He knows in his heart of hearts, that the cold, deliberate killing of a man by his fellow man brutalizes the killers—and that is all society—just as much as it ends human life. Perhaps the killers suffer more harm than the killed.—*The Memphis Press*.

MOORE IS AGAINST CAPITAL PUNISHMENT.

"Capital punishment is a relic of the days when men were forced to trod red-hot ploughshares to prove their innocence," said John Trotwood Moore, Tennessee's distinguished novelist, talking on the subject last night.

"I do not believe in taking a man's life for having committed a crime. That is a barbarous custom, a relic of ancient days. We must be progressive, and more humane toward our fellow-mortals.

"It seems to me that in a Christian land, with all our boasted Christianity, we should practice such, and abolish this terrible method of punishment.

"Capital punishment does not prevent crime. We make use of it in Tenneseee, yet murders are continually committed. Why not try the other method?

"When a man's life is taken at the end of a rope, or in the electric chair, his usefulness is done for. He is of no value to the State, or to society.

"Now if such men were placed in the penitentiary they would have to work for the State, and be of concrete value to the State. In the same time such a man might reform while in prison, and be a factor for good in that institution.

"There is the case of Cole Younger. When a boy his father was killed by bushwhackers, and he entered into killing others. When surrender was declared they refused to let Cole Younger surrender. Later he was placed in the penitentiary. There he proved to be a model prisoner, and won the love of all about him.

"In fact he was so industrious, and so perfect in conduct that he won the sympathy of all wardens under whom he served, until the mater was called to the attention of the Chief Executive of that State, and when put to the people as to whether Cole Younger should be pardoned, after having served twenty-five years for the State, it was overwhelmingly decided that he should have his life and liberty.

Today that man is a good citizen, and has even become the president of a railroad. He gave twenty-five years of his life to the State—was that not enough? Now, isn't he of better use to humanity in general than if his life had been snapped out?

"I think that we should allow our women to vote, for by so doing our laws would become more humane. I think that if women had the ballot in Tennessee this barbarous custom would be speedily abolished. And I sincerely hope that this session of the Legislature will work to that end.—*Nashville Tennessean and American*, January 26, 1913.

JUDGE R. H. PRESCOTT, ONE OF THE LEADING CRIMINAL LAWYERS OF THE SOUTH.

Mr. Duke C. Bowers, Dresden, Tenn.:

DEAR SIR:—I am in receipt of your request that I give you my views concerning Capital Punishment, as now provided by the statutory enactments of our State.

In reply will say that as a penalty for the infraction of the law I believe it to be a failure. In the very face of the most extreme punishment more murders are committed yearly in the United States than ever before, especially in the history of the large American cities and the territory adjacent to them. It does not prohibit; it never has; it never will. The man who kills with cool, deliberate purpose and premeditation moved by malice does not pause to reflect upon the consequences of his act, and the fact that it is written in the law that murder in the first degree shall be punished by death by hanging is no deterrent or restraint to him. In fact, I am constrained from many years' practice in the Criminal Court to believe that punishment of all kinds do not restrain from an infraction of the law, except in the rarest instances. I am of the opinion that the impulse to commit crime is in the blood, like some dissease that lurks in the human body, and is nurtured by the infirmities and frailties of human nature.

On the other hand, often a good citizen is impelled, by sudden impulse of passion, to perpetrate violence against the person of his fellowman. Not one criminal in ten thousand stops to consider the consequences of his act.

After all *there is no law* or its enforcement save that reposed in and reflected by the virtues and patriotism of the masses of the people. And capital punishment does not add to or stimulate either of these characteristics. To take life, even by authority of law, is abhorrent to the better feelings and ideas of justice of the average man. Down in his heart he has an idea that it is wrong—that it is a bloody, cruel, surviving relic of the past ages wherein men were sought to be ruled by power of might and not right. Humane methods of government have advanced with civilization. As a rule, men are more humane, kind and gentle.

I do not touch on the *moral right* to take human life by operation of law. That is a question that must appeal to each individual. I do not believe we have the right as a government to execute one of our citizens. History teaches that it had its origin in revenge. In the early history of England the next of kin to the deceased had the right to pursue and kill the assailant. This give way to a kind of tribal court.

It is interesting to study the origin of capital punishment. The Mosaic Law, as to that, is but a reflection of the custom of the times, and but an expression of the customs of previous ages. In my opinion there was no divine sanction for it.

Again, mistakes have been made and clearly demonstrated, in verdicts of guilt, but too late to do any good, because the defendant had paid the unjust penalty.

I am enclosing a copy of a poem, by Ella Wheeler Wilcox, on the subject of capital punishment. It is the best I have seen.

Wishing you success in your movement, I remain yours very truly, R. H. PRESCOTT.

To the Editor of the Banner

In your issue of January 30, you publish, in your Forum of the People, a letter from A. A. North. I would thank you to publish this reply, hoping that he will see it, and that it will convince him that there is logic as well as sentiment in the proposed movement to do away with capital punishment in Tennessee.

Mr. North apparently thinks that we should not be controlled by sentiment and sympathy, yet if he will investigate all of the great movements that have done more to civilize all nations he will find that these two great motive powers have had much to do with it.

But I am willing to discount these considerations and place my argument before him on a sound basis of logic, reason and statistics. Many men believe that one fact is worth a hundred analogies, and, like Mr. North, insist on knowing "how it works" before they will give up the old for the new. And some are even so constituted that offering undeniable facts to controvert their position will even then fail to put their minds in harmony with the spirit of progress. The idea of the abolishment of the death penalty is no new theory, and has been in practice for a number of years in many States and countries. Former Warden Hatch, of the Michigan State prison, said: *"Michigan is a poor shibboleth for capital punishment advocates,* for it is about the only State in the Union that shows a decided falling off in the criminal populations. *I believe it impossible to reinstate the law authorizing the death-penalty in this State.* The civilized world is tending toward the abolition of the law of death for crime, and the number of executions is constantly decreasing. In this country the States of Kansas, Maine, Michigan, Rhode Island and Wisconsin have abolished the death penalty, and the statistics show that in those States for the last decade and more crimes and criminals have been on a decrease.

In the State of Rhode Island, according to the statistics of the Bureau of Census, there was but five homicides in that State to each 100,000 population; while in the State of Connecticut, which is an adjoining State, and similar in conditions, there were eight homicides to every 100,000. In the State of Maine there were only 2.2 homicides to a population of 100,000, while in the State of Vermont, which is very similar to the State of Maine, there was 7.6 homicides to every 100,000 population. These same statistics hold good throughout the entire list of the States that have abolished capital punishment.

Again, when people are imbued with the value of life as taught them by the example and precept of the State that human life is sacred, they will themselves appreciate that value more than ever. To show the effects of the two methods of dealing with murderers, statistics have been compiled as to the number of convictions in Rhode Island, as compared with Massachusetts and Connecticut, for various periods. In Connecticut it was shown that from the year 1850 to 1880 there were ninety-seven persons tried for murder in the first degree, and but thirteen of that number or a little over 13 per cent, wre convicted as charged. In Massachusetts from 1862 to 1882, a twenty-year period, the number tried for murder in the first degree was 170, with twenty-nine convictions, or 17 per cent of the number tried. But the convictions in Rhode Island, in thirty years after the abolishment of the punishment of death, numbered 63 per cent of the number tried. Thus experience speaks with no uncertain voice as to the advisability of abolishing the penalty of death. Reason adds her plea to mercy in demanding a more sensible and humane method of dealing with felons, and there seems to be no good reason why every man should not work to have our present Legislature pass the enactment amending the present law of the death penalty.

Mr. North makes the statement that the fear of death is a strong deterrent for crime, but this apparently has not proven true in Tennessee, for capital crimes in this State are not on the decrease, but on the increase. Every man knows before he commits any crime that there is a penalty attached, but that apparently does not deter him. In order to arrive at a correct conclusion to Mr. North's argument, we must try to see the case from the viewpoint of the murderer himself. If any man takes the time necessary for deliberation to make his crime murder in the first degree, what is likely to be his line of thought? Will the penalty attached as a punishment enter at all into his consideration of the case?

That depends upon the character of the man, the degree of his malignity, or the intensity of his purpose. There are some men so constituted that they would scarcely give a serious thought to the probable result of their actions. A determination to have revenge, or whatever their object might be, would overcome every other consideration, and they would carry out their evil purpose, no matter whether the punishment be burning at the stake, or simply a fine and imprisonment.

Others, and perhaps the large majority, would think of the threatened punishment. Suppose they do, knowing that a severe penalty is attached will not remove their evil desire to commit the deed. It ismply puts them to devising ways and means to escape detection. When they have settled this to their satisfaction, they will no more hesitate to perpetrate the deed than they would if there were no punishment, because they have convinced themselves that they can escape the legal penalty. Today many of our jurors have a personal prejudice against capital punishment, and many men who would have been convicted for life imprisonment as the penalty, are dismissed without punishment. The man who has nothing but the fear of punishment between him and murder, has only the chance of escape to consider. When he has this arranged to suit himself, the act will be committed, because what matters it to him whether the punishment be light or severe, so long as he confidently expects to escape the penalty entirely? One of the greatest criminologists the world has known, Beccaria, says:

"Perpetual slavery has in it all that is necessary to deter the most hardened and determined as much as has the punishment of death. I say it has more. There are men who can look upon death with intrepidity and firmness, some through fanactism, others through vanity, which attend us even to the grave, others from a desperate resolution to get rid of their misery, and cease to live."

Life has strong claims upon the healthy, the industrious, the happy and the good, but to the diseased, the indolent, the poverty-stricken and the vicious, it is oftentimes a sad mixture, with more misery than pleasure, and is frequently regarded more as a curse to be thrown off, than as a blessing to be cherished. Lord Byron is said to have decleared that he had never known more than twelve happy days in all his life. The United States mortality statistics show that in the cause of death the annual average for homicides from the year 1900 to 1909 was 1608, but the annual average from suicides 5,560, thus showing that the fear of death is no argument to those who have the intention of committing murder.

The sentiment of every enlightened people is against the infliction of the death penalty, whether they are conscious of the fact or not, they will raise doubts not testified by the evidence, to avoid assuming the responsibility of condemning a fellow-creature to death, a responsibility which most men feel is too great for erring man to take upon himself. It has been estimated that in Chicago one man out of every fifty-four tried for murder in the first degree is made to suffer the penalty.

Mr. North brings in the argument of mob law. I would like to quote him Horace Greelye's objection to capital punishment on this point. "I dread human fallibility. Men are prejudiced, passionate, and too often irrational. Today they shout 'Hosanna,' and tomorrow howl 'Crucify Him.' I would save them from the harsher consequences of their own frenzy. Our Savior is by no means a solitary example of the unjust execution of the innocent and just. We have recorded instances of innocent men convicted of murder on their own confession, of men convicted, sentenced and hung for offenses whereof they were in on wise guilty. Men may suffer unjustly, even though death be stricken from the list of our legal penalties. So long as man is liable to error, I would have him reserve the possibility of correcting his mistake, and correcting the wrong he has been led into perperating."

In speaking of life imprisonment, Mr. North says: "Prison bars may be sawed in two, pardons may be obtained." If Mr. North will investigate the statistics of our own State prison he will find that eighty-nine per cent of those given a life sentence die in that institution; that only five and three-tenths per cent are pardoned, and five and seven-tenths per cent of life terms are commuted. He will also find that in the history of that institution that there has never been a life prisoner to escape.

Therefore he has based much of his letter on statements that he cannot substantiate, and I personally would like to meet Mr. North and submit to him even more statistics; and many more arguments, against capital punishment than I can place in this letter because I know that I have even now imposed on your good nature and have occupied a bit more space than I should.

HENRY W. LEWIS.

SIX REASONS.

WHY CAPITAL PUNISHMENT SHOULD BE ABOLISHED.

REASON NO. 1.

It does not deter the commission of murder. There are fewer murdes per capita in states which have abolished the death sentence—as in Maine and Wisconsin—than in New York and Pennsylvania, which still retain it.

REASON NO. 2.

Innocent individuals are occasionally executed, which makes the State a murder of the worst kind. Capital punishment prevents reparation in cases of subquently proven innocence.

REASON NO. 3.

Two or more men, organized under a form of government, have no more right to take life than one man has. It is murder in either case, and brutalizing in both.

REASON NO. 4.

It is certainly a relic of barbarism. To abolish it would be a step forward. As civilization has advanced, punishment has always become less severe and crime has also become less common.

REASON NO. 5.

Capital punishment usually deprives the criminal of the one due which civilized society owes its unfortunate children of this class—the chance for spiritual reformation and expiation to prepare for the hereafter.

REASON NO. 6.

Life improsionment is a severer and juster punishment for a murderer than to be given early his earthly quietus. Those States which sanction legal murder do more—they murder civilization.

EXTRACT.

Because the majority of men sentenced to death petition for a commutation to life imprisonment, is not by any means, conclusive evidence that death is a more severe punishment, nor that it acts as a stronger deterent. As a whole, I am inclined to think to give a life sentence would do more good than the infliction of the death penalty. Like extracting a tooth, we put

it off as long as possible and really suffer more than if we had had the tooth pulled when it first pained us. So with a life prisoner, as a deterent. He takes the life sentence in preference to hanging. Had he been hanged the matter would have been forgotten, but while in prison he is a continuing example to keep others from committing crime and meeting a like fate. Besides if it developes he is innocent he can be freed and at all events he will be given time to reform and expiate his crime and prepare for the hereafter.

PRISONERS DO NOT CONTEMTLATE ANY PUNISHMENT.... ..

As a matter of fact, criminals who commit infamous crimes, commit them under circumstances, by which they expect to escape detection or capture entirely. I remember within 16 months, four men who had committed murder, in Weakley County, Tenn., escaped and neither has ever been apprehended. We should have better facilities in Tennessee for catching criminals and make the law against procuring and carrying the means with which to commit murder, adequate to restrict the use of deadly weapons; then have Jury Commissions for each County and make punishment swift and certain for crimes in Tennessee and crimes will diminish.

EXTRACT FROM AGUMENT AGAINST THE DEATH PENALTY

While we submit that where the equities are equal, the element of mercy should hold the balance of power in deciding this question, we would not have appealed to you on that ground, had not a certain Attorney-General, with a master hand pictured, in an article in the Nashville papers of the 1st inst., the awful suffering and remorse of the family o fthe vicitm of a homicide. Now we agree that it is hard on the family of the deceased and our sympathy goes out to them, whether his death was the result of an assassination or a justifiable homicide it is all the same to them in either case. But for that reason would you have two widows, two sets of orphans and two sorrowing parents? Why, the family of the prisoner are just as innocent of an offense as the family of the deceased, and are just as much entitled to compassion and sympathy. For example, a man commits murder. He probably got drunk or was by environment made a criminal. He has a good wife and also children; a good mother and father and a large number of relatives, all innocent people and profoundly grieved that the offense was committed. The accused is tried and convicted and sentenced to be hanged. The very thoughts of taking the life of the husband, father, brother and son breaks a multitude of hearts. The time has healed the wounds that grief for the victim rent, but as the days roll by and the time approaches for the execution of the prisoner the heart of the mother and father all but breaks; the affectionate and tender cord of love that stretches from the altar to the scaffold is crushed but not broken, and the heart of the wife once gay is burned to its very socket. She goes to and from the awful death sell. Little innocent hearts of children are crushed like the tender blades of grass, beneath the angry wheels of cannon on the Turkish battlefield, yet they are all innocent. The brother and sister suffer for his sins, and see his ghost-like form in their dreams of repose. As the day draws near the father and mother with tottering footsteps visit the death cell, and their minds won der back to the time when a little boy said his prayers at his mother's knee and whistled the tune that his father carrolled and they ask God "why they have this affliction to bear." The wife, children and relatives and friends all bid him goodby and leave with breaking hearts, "bitterly thinking of tomorrow." With heart-breaking despair, the mother prays God to spare her child, and as the time fiyes by the height of heaven could not measure her sorrow. The father's hair turns gray over night, and the very souls all are scarred and forever seared over by the thought of the vengeance visited on their unfortunate relative, son and husand and father. The parents are hurried to their graves of broken hearts, the wife tries to forget, but cannot forgive and the hearts of the children, relatives and friends are hardened by the harrowing example of killing by the State. Two families are in mourning and the prisoner's family crushed and heart broken by a protracted suspense, and that amounts to cruelty to the innocents. Then why make two families instead of one desolate? Then suppose he was innocent? The State cannot retract what it has done. If life imprsonment would serve the same purpose, would you not prefer it to the death penalty.

The French painter has depicted a weired but striking picture. In the dreary hours of night Napoleon's drummer boy is made to arise and sound the march. The ghost of Napoleon comes forward and stands attention; and then the Grand Army and the Old Guard pass by in solemn review before the "Arch Angel of War." They come from Arcola, from Lodi, from Australitz, from Waterloo. As you are considering the passage of this law, the blood of the many martyrs of the block, the gillotine and the gibet appeal to you to abolish the law that is founded on vengeance and destruction instead of mercy and reform.

CRIMES AND THEIR PENALTIES.

Compiled From the Codes or Revised Statutes of the Several States as Amended by Subsequent Legislation.

Murder in the first degree, in the table below, may be generally defined to be the unlawful, intentional and premeditated killing of a human being, or such a killing resulting from the commission or attempt to commit one of the graver crimes, such as arson, burglary, rape or robbery.

Alabama—For murder, first degree, death or life imprisonment; robbery, death or not less than 10 years; rape, death or not less than 10 years; arson, first degree, death or not less than 10 years.

Alaska—For murder, first degree, death or life imprisonment; robbery, 1 to 15 years; rape, 3 to 20 years; arson, first degree, 10 to 20 years.

Arizona—For murder, first degree, death or life imprisonment; robbery, not less than 5 years; rape, not less than 5 years and up to life; arson, first degree, not less than 2 years.

Arkansas—For murder, first degree, death; robbery, 3 to 21 years; rape, death to 10 years; arson, first degree, 2 to 10 years.

California—For murder, first degree, death or life imprisonment; robbery, not les than 1 year; rape, not less than 5 years; arson, first degree, not less than 2 years.

Colorado—For murder, first degree, death or life imprisonment; robbery, 3 to 14 years; rape, 1 to 20 years; arson, first degree, 1 to 10 years.

Connecticut—For murder, first degree, death; robbery, not over 7 years; rape, not over 30 years; arson, first degree, not over 10 years.

Delaware—For murder, first degree, death; robbery, not over 12 years; rape, death or life imprisonment; arson, first degree, death.

Florida—For murder, first degree, death; robbery, not over 20 years; rape, death or life imprisonment; arson, first degree, any term up to life.

Georgia—For murder, first degree, death or life imprisonment; robbery, 4 to 20 years; rape, death or 1 to 20 years; arson, first degree, 5 to 20 years.

Idaho—For murder, first degree, death or life imprisonment; robbery, not less than 5 years and up to life; rape, not less than 5 years and up to life; arson, first degree, not less than 2 years and up to life.

Illinois—For murder, first degree, death or not less than 14 years and up to life; robbery, 1 year and up to life; rape, 1 year and up to life; arson, 1 to 20 years.

Indiana—For murder, first degree, death or life imprisonment; robbery, 2 to 14 years, $1,000; rape 2 to 21 years; arson, first degree, 2 to 21 years

Iowa—For murder, first degree, death or life imprisonment; robbery, 10 to 20 years; rape, any term up to life; arson, first degree, any term up to life.

Kansas—For murder, first degree, life imprisonment; robbery, 10 to 21 years; rape, 5 to 21 years; arson, first degree, 10 to 21 years.

Kentucky—For murder, first degree, death or life imprisonment; robbery, 2 to 10 years; rape, death or 10 to 20 years; arson, first degree 10 to 20 years.

Louisiana—For murder, first degree, death; robbery, not over 14 years; rape, death; arson, first degree, death

Maine—For murder, first degree, life imprisonment; robbery, any term of years; rape, any term of years; arson, first degree, life.

Maryland—For murder, first degree. death; robbery, 3 to 10 years; rape. death or 18 months to 21 years; arson, first degree, death or not over 20 years.

Massachusetts—For murder, first degree, death; robbery, life imprisonment; rape. life imprisonment or any term of years; arson, first degree, life imprisonment or any term of years.

Michigan—For murder, first degree, life imprisonment; robbery, life imprisonment or any term of years; rape, life imprisonment or any term of years; arson. first degree, life imprisonment or any term of years.

Minnesota—For murder, first degree, death; robbery, 5 to 40 years; rape, 7 to 30 years; arson, first degree, not less than 10 years.

Mississippi—For murder, first degree, death or life imprisonment; robbery, not over 15 years; rape and first-degree arson, death or life imprisonment.

Missouri—For murder, first degree, death or life imprisonment; robbery, not less than 5 years; rape, death or not less than 5 years; arson, first degree, not less than 5 years.

Montana—For murder, first degree, death or life imprisonment; robbery, 1 to 20 years; rape, not less than 5 years; arson, first degree. not less than 5 years.

Nebraska—For murder, first degree, death or life imprisonment; robbery, 3 to 15 years; rape, 3 to 20 years; arson, first degree, 1 to 20 years.

Nevada—For murder, first degree, death or life imprisonment; robbery, not less than 5 years; rape, not less than 5 years and up to life; arson. first degree, not less than 2 years and up to life.

New Hampshire—For murder, first degree, death or life imprisonment; robbery, not over 30 years; rape, not over 30 years; arson, first degree, not over 30 years.

New Jersey—For murder, first degree, death; robbery, 15 years or $1,000, or both; rape, $5.000 or both; arson, first degree, $2,000 or both.

New York—For murder, first degree, death; robbery, not over 20 years; rape. not over 20 years; arson, first degree, not over 40 years.

North Carolina—For murder, first degree. death; robbery, no statutory definition; rape. death; arson, first degree, death.

North Dakota—For murder, first degree, death or life imprisonment; robbery, not less than 1 year; rape, not less than 10 years; arson, first degree, not less than 10 years.

Ohio—For murder, first degree, death or life imprisonment; robbery, 1 to 15 years; rape, 3 to 20 years; arson, first degree, not over 20 years.

Oklahoma—For murder, first degree, death or life imprisonment; robbery, not less than 10 years; rape, not less than 10 years; arson, first degree, 20 to 30 years.

Oregon—For murder, first degree, death; robbery, not less than 10 years and up to life; rape, 3 to 20 years; arson, first degree, 10 to 20 years.

Pennsylvania—For murder, first degree, death; robbery, not over 10 years and $1,000; rape, not over 15 years and $1,000; arson, first degree, not over 20 years and $4,000.

Rhode Island—For murder, first degree, life imprisonment; robbery, not less than 5 years and up to life; rape, not less than 10 years and up to life; arson, first degree, not less than 10 years and up to life.

South Carolina—For murder, first degree, death or life imprisonment; robbery, no statutory definition; rape, death or life imprisonment; arson, first degree, death or not less than 10 years.

South Dakota—For murder, first degree, death or life imprisonment; robbery, 10 to 20 years; rape, not less than 10 years; arson, first degree, not less than 10 years.

Tennessee—For murder, first degree, death; robbery, 5 to 15 years; rape, death or not less than 10 years and up to life; arson, first degree, 5 to 21 years.

Texas—For murder, first degree, death or life imprisonment; robbery, not less than 5 years and up to life; rape, death or any term over 5 years up to life; arson, first degree, 5 to 20 years.

Utah—For murder, first degree, death or life imprisonment; robbery, not less than 5 years and up to life; rape, not less than 5 years; arson, first degree, 2 to 15 years.

Vermont—For murder, first degree, death or life imprisonment; robbery, not over 20 years and $1,000; rape, not over 20 years or $2,000, or both; arson, first degree, any term up to life.

Virginia—For murder, first degree, death; robbery, death or 8 to 18 years; rape, death or 5 to 20 years; arson, first degree, death.

Washington—For murder, first degree, death or life imprisonment; robbery, not less than 5 years; rape, not less than 5 years; arson, first degree, not less than 5 years.

West Virginia—For murder, first degree, death or life imprisonment; robbery, not less than 10 years; rape, death or 7 to 20 years; arson, first degree, death or life imprisonment.

Wisconsin—For murder, first degree, life imprisonment; robbery, 3 to 10 years; rape, 10 to 30 years; arson, first degree, 7 to 14 years.

Wyoming—For murder, first degree, death; robbery, not over 14 years; rape, not less than 1 year and up to life; arson, first degree, not over 21 years.

LYNCHINGS AND LEGAL EXECUTIONS.

Lynchings—The total number of lynchings in the United States from 1885 to November 15. 1912, was 3,413. In 1912, to November 15, there were 52 lynchings, of which 49 occurred in the South and 3 in the North; 49 were males and 3 females. Of the lynched, 50 were negroes and 2 whites. The offenses for which they were lynched were: Rap,, 10; murder, 26; attempted rape, 2; insults to white women, 3; unknown causes, 1; robbery and assault, 1; race prejudice, 1; arson, 3; complicity in murder. 3; murderous assaults, 2. The States in which the lynchings occurred and the number in each were as follows: Alabama, 5; Arkansas. 3; Florida, 3; Georgia, 11; Louisiana, 4; Mississippi, 5; Montana, 1; North Carolina, 1; North Dakota, 1; Oregon, 1; Virginia, 1; West Virginia. 1; Wyoming, 1; Oklahoma, 1; Pennsylvania, 5; South Carolina, 5; Texas, 3.

Legal Executions—In 1908, to November 15, there were 92; in 1909 there were 107; in 1910 there were 104; in 1911 there were 61; and in 1912. to November 15, there were 128. of which 62 were in the North and 66 in the South; 89 were whites and 39 were colored; 127 were males and 1 female. The crimes for which they were executed were: Murder, 125; rape, 3. The States in which the executions in 1912, to November 15, took place, and the number in each. were as follows: Alabama, 4; Arkansas, 8; Calofirnia, 4; Connecticut. 2; Colorado, 1; Florida, 3; Georgia, 9; Illinois, 6; Kentucky, 4; Massachusetts, 5; Maryland, 1: Mississippi, 7; Missouri, 1; New York, 21: New Jersey, 4; North Carolina, 4; Nevada, 2; Ohio, 1; Pennsylvania, 6; South Carolina, 5; Tennes

see, 9; Texas, 4; Utah, 6; Vermont, 1; Washington, 2; Wyoming, 2; Virginia. 6.—*From a table prepared by Geo. P. Upton, Chicago, Ill.*

APPENDIX.

TO ABOLISH DEATH PENALTY.

C. C. GILBERT, OF DAVIDSON.

"As long as the human race will be called to sit in judgment over a fellow creature and are sworn to decide whether he must die, the death penalty must be a question of urgent interest and one upon which every man should form an intelligent opinion." The above statement was made by the Hon. C. C. Gilbert, member of the Legislature from Davidson County, who will, Tuesday, introduce a bill to abolish the death penalty.

"The more I study this problem, the more I am convinced that to punish murder by death is wrong," continued Mr. Gilbert. "If a man's judgment could possibly be infallible then a remote excuse for capital punishment might exist. Looking at this subject from one viewpoint it seems incredible that in this wonderful age, when civilization is reaching its highest point in the history of man, that the same spirit of revenge that existed when the human race was still in its infancy should still control the people of Tennessee in their treatment of its most unfortunate class.

"All that is needed to erase the punishment of death from our statutes is to get our citizens to throw aside their prejudice long enough to examine the case fairly and intelligently. As Wendell Phillip says: 'To get men to listen is half the battle, and the hardest half in all reforms.' Many persons never investigate a subject with any other purpose than to strengthen the opinions and prejudice they already hold. It is a fact that a large majority of those who have studied this subject fairly are impressed with doubts of the righteousness of the death penalty, sufficient, at least, to excuse them from service on juries for murder trials— if, indeed, they are not fully convinced that hanging men for crime is in itself a crime.

"In the most primitive state of society retaliation was the

method of punishing offences, and this was inflicted by the one who suffered the injury or by some of his friends the punishment of death, according to Agassiz, Darwin, Humboldt, and other noted scientists, is of heathen and savage origin and it is a lamentable fact that Tennessee still adheres to this barbarian idea. Among primitive people the death penalty was most likely inflicted by stoning, as stones were about the most convenient and effective death dealing weapons they possessed. After stoning, came burning, and it was long years after before an instrument was made by which a man could be beheaded.

"In the days of Blackstone, there were in England one hundred and sixty offences punishable by death, and at one time they reached two hundred and twenty-three. Within the memory of many yet living it was the law of England to hang persons convicted of stealing goods to the value of five shillings from a store, warehouse or stable, while the person convicted of treason should have his bowels torn out and burned while he was yet alive.

"Imprisonment for debt was the law in every state of the union except five as late as 1845. A case in the Pennsylvania reports is cited to show where a man was actually imprisoned thirty days for two cents. It is hardly necessary to speak of the nineteen persons who were executed in this country under the law because they had gone into league with satan and practiced witchcraft. The early history of Tennessee relates such a case occurring in this state.

"There are many good men and women in Tennessee who are constantly agitating the work of reform in penal jurisprudence and great progress is being made toward humane, sensible and effective means of dealing with those who are in danger of falling into the criminal class. And today there is a growing sentiment among law-makers to hold a post-mortem over antiquated and obsolete methods and statutes. Laws, when outgrown by civilization should be declared legally dead.

"Without any apology for crime or unworthy sympathy for the criminal, it can be said that justice as well as mercy should make great allowance for human conduct. No human mind is able to decide how far any man may justly be held for his acts. Every man who has been immuned in prison walls or suffered death at the hand of his fellow was once an innocent, helpless babe. His whole life may have been one continuous struggle against disease, against poverty and trying circumstances, against temptation thrown in his way by society and perhaps against his own natural inclination to do evil.

"Reason speaks with no uncertain voice as to the advisability of abolishing the death penalty and in demanding a more humane method of dealing with felons, and it seems to me there can be no good reason why every man should not oppose the cruel law and why this present Legislature should not erase it from the statute books of Tennessee. Capital punishment is a disgrace to our age, to our race, to our civilization. When society insists that it must still strangle some of its members in order to impress others with the value of life, that it must teach people the sacredness of life by maintaining a school of murder, it confesses itself a lamentable failure and a pretentious fraud. I, for one, will give the best of my ability to aid in amending our present laws on the death penalty."—*Nashville Tennessean and American.*

DUKE C. BOWERS' ARGUMENT AGAINST CAPITAL PUNISHMENT.

The first case of murder of which we have any record was that of Cain killing Abel. In this instance God himself was the judge, the jury, and the whole court. He did not put Cain to death, neither would he allow the people to do it.

In God's commandment to man he said: "Thou shalt not kill." There were some man-made laws after this that stated: "An eye for an eye and a tooth for a tooth"—likewise a life for a life; but these same Mosaic laws made it a capital offense to pick up sticks on the Sabbath.

Christ came and changed the old law, "an eye for an eye," declaring that vengeance belonged to God. He also taught that it was better to do good than evil on the Sabbath. The difference in the teaching of Moses and Christ was that Moses shed his enemies' blood, while Christ shed His own blood for His enemies.

Imprisoning a person and trying to reform him exemplifies the teachings of Christ to overcome evil with good; while taking one's life is wreaking vengeance, and vengeance is the Lord's so saith Jesus.

Because we are Southerners is no reason why we should favor lynching or hanging. Christianity should be the same all over the country. Life belongs to God in the South as well as in the North. "The Lord giveth and the Lord taketh away" should apply to the whole world.

Ella Wheeler Wilcox says, "Thought breeds thought," and this power of suggestion is strongly illustrated in a story ex-Warden Rice tells. A hanging took place one morning at the Nashville penitentiary; all was gloom about the prison; yet that very afternoon a prisoner slipped up behind a fellow prisoner and killed him.

Who is able to say whether or not the murder committed in the morning by the state did or not put the idea into the man's head to commit the second murder?

Some people argue that if capital punishment is abolished crime will increase. Brand Whitlock tells in his lecture, "Thou shalt not steal," that in the debate of the House of Lords on the bill to abolish the death penalty for stealing from a dwelling to the amount of 40 shillings, Lord Chief Justice Ellenborough declared that if the bill passed, the property of every householder in the kingdom would be left wholly without protection, but his Lord-ship's fears have not been justified in England.

The experience of those of our states that have abolished capital punishment proves that if anything deters capital offenses, it is by the state not doing what it says its citizens shall not do. Burning at the stake did not prevent the spread of the Christian religion. If putting people to death could not stop a righteous cause, how can you expect it to stop an unrighteous one?

From a statistical standpoint, as gathered from the United States Mortality Report in the states reporting for ten years previous to 1910, those in which capital punishment prevails show one and one-half times as many homicides per 100,000 population as against those states that do not have capital punishment. For 1909, the last year reported, those states that have capital pun-ishment had two and one-fourth times as many homicides as did the states in which capital punishment does not obtain.

Another, and perhaps the strongest argument against capital punishment, is that the innocent are sometimes hanged. Following is a letter I received a few days ago from a friend·

COLUMBUS, KY., FEB. 7, 1913.

Mr. Duke C. Bowers, Dresdent, Tenn ·

Dear Duke—I will try and state a case to you that Mr. Otis Peebles told me happened in Milburn some years ago. Two negroes by the name of Duvall and Clapp were arrested for rape on a white woman by the name of Warden. She could not state whether her assailants were white or black. They tried, convicted and hanged the two negroes at Blandville, Ky., Their last words were that they were innocent of the crime. Some years later a white man by the name of Gossop moved to Arkansas from Milburn, and shortly afterwards took sick, and on his deathbed made confession to the crime. But two innocent lives' had gone to meet their Maker.

Your friend,
HARRY PEARSON.

Now, if life imprisonment had been the maximum punishment in the above case, then these two men could have been given their liberty and the state would not bear the stain of having murdered two innocent men. Isn't it better that ninety-nine guilty ones' lives should be saved than for one innocent life to be taken?

Rev. J. O. McClurkan of this city told me that he had talked with nearly every person that has been hanged here in the past fifteen years, and that according to his judgment, there were only about three or four cases out of the whole bunch in which there were no mitigating circumstances.

Some people are against capital punishment because of the pardoning power resting in the Governor's hand. Warden Rimmer of the state penitentiary at Nashville wrote me that within the past ten years 151 life prisoners have been received; of this number only seven have been pardoned and ten commuted, leaving 88 4-5 per cent to serve out their time.

Anyone familiar with the courts of our state knows that a great number of men who would make good jurors are disqualified from service on account of their conviction on the subject of capital punishment. To abolish the death penalty would, to my mind, give the speedier convictions, save money for the state, be more in keeping with the progressive spirit of this era and be the best advertisement the State of Tennessee could procure.

There are people in the North who think that we of the South are a lot of hot-heads, blood-thirsty murderers. Let us abolish capital punishment and show these people that they are mistaken. It will be the biggest boost Tennessee ever had. I believe it will help to bring capital and investors into our midst. Let's quit employing a man to hang people—rather let us give them to understand that we want them to take a man and reform him.

Believing that my judgment is right in this matter, I appeal to you to rally to the support of Mr. Gilbert and his bill to abolish capital punishment in Tennessee.

DUKE C. BOWERS.

Editor The News Scimitar:

The campaign being waged before the Tennessee Legislature by Mr. Bowers, of Memphis, and others, has aroused much interest throughout the state and elsewhere. In nearly every newspaper in Tennessee communications are printed as often as the papers themselves appear. All of which is well. So far as the writer of this is concerned, he has never cared to go deeper in his antagonism to capital punishment than the conviction long held that no community of men has a right to go further than an individual, and that neither community nor individual has a right to take from a man that which God gave him, and which he is entitled to retain until God's finger of finality touches him and he gives it back.

Nearly two thousand years ago the Old Testament became a back number, an interesting but obsolete reminder of an era when men were in the formative state, and needed the supreme penalty for mundane misdeeds. Since that time there has come the New Testament, God's latest pronouncement, making love and mercy the basis of men's deeds. We have long been growing away from capital punishment.

No more than four generations ago, in England, the world's

most progressive and advanced nation, there were a hundred or more crimes which called by laws for the death penalty. These have one by one been changed, until today only murder and treason, save perhaps in war times, are punishable by death. In many other countries, even the murder of a sovereign calls for nothing severer than life imprisonment. A few years ago in our Western States, when Isolated communities were their own law-makers, horse and cattle thieves always left the country by the noose route. Certain states have recently done what Tennessee is considering, abolished the death penalty entirely. Statistics show that in those states the crime of murder has diminished instead of increased. The theory is that the convicted criminal has the chance of being prepared for eternity. It also secures to the convicted one the privilege of a restoration to liberty in the event that exculpatory evidence later comes to light. In 50 per cent at least of murder convictions there is the possibility of juries' errors, either as to the guilt at all of the defendant, or as to the actual degree of his guilt. This percentage of uncertainty is itself sufficient to relegate the custom, were that the only argument against it.

It is no surprise to find a majority of lawyers against Mr. Bowers in his fight. Lawyers, and there's a pity to it, become, from their earliest legal training, inoculated with the virus of precedents and custom. I call it virus because it has been a bane to society. There is as much wrong done society and the law by the antiquated and obstinate adherence of the legal profession to precedents and procedures as by any one class of criminals in the world. You may shake up the profession, but you can't wake it up. It's for the people, with visions unrestrained and minds free, to do the work of radicalism in lawmaking.

I don't know whether the present Legislature will abolish capital punishment or not. I do know that some future Legislature will, if this one fails. And it will be for two reasons:

First, that it is not necessary as a preventive of murder; and,

Second, because it is an unholy and a barbarous crime in itself. WALTER CAIN.

Gen. N. M. Curtis, in his speech before Congress to abolish the death penalty, among other things, said: "Those who claim it to be our duty to continue the law of past ages are of the same class of men Sir Thomas More spoke of as those 'who thought it a moral sin to be wiser than their grandfathers.' They have lived in every age, valiant defendants of established customs and laws. They suppressed Galileo Galilei, and sent him to a dungeon, 'guilty of having seen the earth revolve around the sun.' "

AGAINST DEATH PENALTY.

Rev. Green P. Jackson Opposes Capital Punishment.

"Capital punishment should never have been used before the coming of Christ, and it is an outrage to civilization that it has been used since then," said Rev. Green P. Jackson, a Methodist minister, who has been preaching in Middle Tennessee for fifty-five years, while talking with a reporter for The Democrat yesterday.

"Man has no right to take what he has not given—man has no right to say to this man, 'Thou shalt die,' when God himself has ordained, 'Thou shalt not kill.'

'When the Christ of Galilee came to earth it was to preach the kingdom of God upon earth—and it was his wish that man should not slay his fellow-man.

"The Son of God suffered the excruciating tortures of capital punishment. Is it not enough that the Son of Man was put to death? Why should we wish to kill men in this day of enlightened civilization?

"It is my hope and prayer that the bill against capital punishment will be passed in this session of the Legislature."

Yesterday Mr. Jackson called upon Duke C. Bowers, of Memphis, who is here to try to get the bill passed, and handed Mr. Bowers a petition signed by some of the most prominent men of the city against capital punishment.—*The Nashville Democrat.*

ABOLISH BARBARISM, SAYS RABBI LEWINTHAL.

"The bill for repealing capital punishment in Tennessee may pass or may not, but it is a good sign of the progress of humanity, justice and civilization. This struggle is not merely a passing sensation—it has been going on for a century, and even if the bill is defeated, the agitation will be resumed," said Rabbi Lewinthal of this city in a masterful sermon against capital punishment a day ago.

"To the credit of the human race it must be said that in every generation and every clime people were anxious to practice justice. Their will was good and their heart craved justice, but the trouble was they were not advanced enough intellectually to know what justice was. They believed they were practicing justice, but in fact they were practicing barbarism. In our days we know better; therefore, let us drop all prejudices and reform our penal codes.

"Let us abolish capital punishment. Just abolish it, and the people of Tennessee will be satisfied. They will be satisfied be cause humanity demands it, justice demands it, experience demands it, and civilization demands it. Away with capital punishment, away with it now, and away with it forever."—*The Nashville Democrat*.

BUSINESS MEN FAVOR ABOLITION OF DEATH PENALTY.

Unanimous endorsement was given by the members of the Nashville Business Men's Association, at the regular meeting Monday night, of the campaign which is being waged before the Legislature for the abolition of capital punishment. H. W. Lewis, M. S. Ross and other members of the association spoke in regard to the bill pending before the Legislature, and told of the good effects obtained where capital punishment has been abolished. *Nashville Tennessean and American*.

EDITORIAL FROM THE LEXINGTON PROGRESS.

Duke C. Bowers, who has residence in the town of Dresden since retirement from active and personal management of the chain of groceries he established and conducted for several years with signal success in the city of Memphis, has been in Nashville since the convention of the Fifty-eighth General Assembly for the sole purpose of pushing to passage if possible a bill abolishing the death penalty and substituting therefor life imprisonment.

Mr. Bowers, prompted by humanity alone, is bearing the whole expense of this work and says that if he can be successful in the Tennessee Legislature he is going to carry the fight before the legislative bodies of all the states in the Union.

He is conducting a vigorous, persistent and intelligent campaign and that his cause is gaining ground is known to all who know the facts as they existed before the convention of the Legislature and at present.

Mr. Bowers shows by statistics that the number of homicides per year is greatest in the states in which the death penalty is inflicted, but he thinks his greatest argument was made by Judge Greer, who spoke before the legislative committee, depicted a legal hanging and at the close asked this question: "Gentlemen of the committee, if Jesus of Nazareth could have looked down on that scene and spoken do you think he would have said, 'Well done, thou good and faithful servant?'" Mr. Bowers says that if his bill passes and is amended by the exception of any crime, it will be like a fellow saying, "Yes, I will get religion—with the sole exception that I will keep on stealing." Mr. Bowers has the help of some of the best members of the Legislature and still others suggest that his plan in the punishment of criminals might safely be given a trial.

VIGOROUS FIGHT AGAINST CAPITAL PUNISHMENT.

An effort is being made to abolish capital punishment in the State of Tennessee, which has brought out very conspicuously that there is a large element of people who oppose the taking of human life for any reason whatever, those holding to this view contending that the individual crime of shedding blood does not justify the shedding of blood on the part of the State as an expiation. They contend that nothing should be taken from a human being that cannot be restored; that only the Giver of Life has the right to take the life of a human being.

The discussion of this question has developed a lofty sentiment among the people. It has shown that in their sober moments and mature judgment they look with horror on the legally sanctioned practice of killing those who kill.

It is commendable in those who are making this fight for

the abolishment of capital punishment that their contention is that the real and only object of the law in punishing criminals is to prevent a repetition of of their crime, and to hold out the punishment of them as object lessons to deter others from committing similar crimes.

These zealous and active opponents of capital punishment take the position that confinement for life, without the hope of pardon or escape, would be just as effective a deterrent to crime as the death penalty. They contend that it is the certainty and not the severity of punishment that is effective in preventing crime, and that if this be true it is the duty of the State to do away with the gallows altogether, and in its stead provide a mode of punishment for atrocious crimes that would be free of the horrors of the gibbet.

Though capital punishment has the sanction of the ages, there is much to be said against it. Divested of all the moods and passions that inflame us in the presence of an atrocious crime, we can with good reason argue the wrong of legal death and show that solitary confinement for life would serve the same end in giving protection to society, but there is a spirit of resentment and a passion for revenge, which, if aroused, leads us to invoke the Mosaic law of "an eye for an eye and a tooth for a tooth."

Whatever policy, with respect to the solution of this problem, may be determined on as wise and expedient for the Legislature to follow, we feel sure the discussion of the question which has been engaged in by a large number of people will have good results, for it has brought out the finest sentiments of the people, showing that they not only want to be just, but merciful as well, and that if they can be both just and merciful in the abolishment of the death penalty they will at least have soothed their own consciences in deferring the taking of human life to a higher power than that which has been created at the hands of man.— *Nashville Tennessean and American.*

OPPOSES CAPITAL PUNISHMENT.

Editor Tennessean and American:

Allow me to say, I heartily approve of your stand against capital punishment. Of course, I am not surprised to find you on this side, as you have always been for the right and against the wrong.

Since I commenced to think about it I have been opposed to capital punishment because, first, it is not the best correction of crime; second, it appears to me a savage practice—a relic of savagery; third, shall the state commit cold-blooded murder to offset the same crime committed by the individual? The latter commits his crime for some real or imaginary grievance; the state does it in the name of civilized law and decency; fourth, as I see it, there is nothing in Christ's teachings that sanctions capital punishment.

His prominent characteristic was that "He did not resent evil," and His example is to be taken as final.

I am praying that this Legislature of Tennessee will do itself the honor to pass a bill abolishing capital punishment.

Martin, Tenn.   REV. J. J. THOMAS.

OPPOSES THE DEATH PENALTY.

Editor Tennessean and American:

As a mother and one who would be rejoiced to see capital punishment done away with, let me say through your columns that I heartily endorse what Mr. Duke C. Bowers and Rev. J. J. Thomas had to say on the subject.

As a people who believe in the religion of the Lord Jesus Christ, let us unite in one strong battle array against capital punishment. Have the lawmakers of a great commonwealth the right to plunge immortal souls into hell—even if under provocation one had committed murder? Give time for repentance.

David, the man after God's own heart, committed murder, and yet, after all, was restored in His sight. And then in the name of her, who in the valley of the shadow of death bore the son her heart cherished so dearly, and whose love can penetrate prison walls, let our legislators do away with capital punishment.

"Am I my brother's keeper?" Yes, and as you seldom hear of the rich, or well-to-do being electrocuted, and as justice sel-

dom reaches the influential; but as the weak and erring, untutored and unprotected, are often the victims of injustice, we pray that imprisonment, say without the chance of pardon, be substituted for death penalty. Life is sweet to even the lower animals. And how much more precious must be the life even of one imprisoned for a life sentence? There is chance of and opportunity for repentance.   MRS. ROBERT E. LINK.
Cottonwood, Tenn.

THE JUDICIARY COMMITTEE HEARINGS.

Judge Greer, of Memphis, opened for the Gilbert bill, the first considered. "I state on the threshold," he said, "that a private citizen of the State has been the most active recent mover in this matter. I have been working on this matter for thirty years. He has done more in thirty days to get it before the Legislature. I wish, therefore, to ask Mr. Duke C. Bowers to either read or make a statement of the faith that has moved him in this humane work."

BOWER'S SUGGESTION.

Mr. Bowers suggested that Judge Greer be heard, and that the committee then postpone the hearing to Tuesday, when there would be more time and other speakers to present the matter. Mr. Bowers referred in this to K. T. McConnico, of Nashville, who sat beside him.

Mr. Bowers' suggestion was followed by Judge Greer, who said in part: "I have come away from the beside of a sick wife, so deeply am I interested in this matter. It is therefore imperative that I must, if I am to speak at all, speak to you now.

"I have been so immensely gratified after all the weary years of waiting at the assurance that there is a probability of this measure, for which I longed since my childish eyes looked for the first and only time on the judicial murder of a fellow-man, becoming a law.

"It has been the longing that has caused me to send to each Legislature a bill to do away with this relic of barbarism. I have been turned down and turned down, but I have seen the thing grow to a point where there is a probability of passage.

"I am not going to put my reasons for this step as mere sentimental reasons. A little reflection will show that the object of punishment is twofold, with a third and subsidiary consideration. First, there is the reason of restraint, to protect society from the man who has outraged it. The second is to deter crime by the example of the punishment. The third has come of late years, to reform the criminal and make him go forth a better man.

"There are some, indeed, who go back to the old law of vengeance, or an eye for an eye, but every thinking man knows that punishment can have but two reasons, protection by restraint and prevention by deterrents.

"If the killing of a man by law served either of these purposes, I would say let them die. But if the figures show, as they incontrovertibly do, that wherever that form of punishment has been abolished and the experiment of milder punishment has been tried, the percentage of homicides has decreased, the percentage of convictions increased. If this is true, gentlemen, that the aim of punishment is better subserved by the milder form, is there any shred of excuse for shedding human blood?

'If this is not true, why have you prohibited public executions? If you wanted to deter by brutality you would see that all saw the executions. If it is right to take life, always there would be volunteers to cut the trap door from under criminals. Can you imagine such a thing?

"You have no public execution because of the horror of it and because of the brutalization of other men witnessing it. If you can deter without shedding blood, why shed it?

"I can tell you something of the horrors of it. I was only a boy. I went to the jail and saw a man brought from the jail in his shroud; saw him sit on his coffin in a wagon and ride a mile through a glorious day to the place of execution.

"With bound arms, he half staggered up to the scaffold. The black cap was put on. The legs were bound. The trap dropped, and the figure dangled in space, arms and legs struggling to rise. Can you imagine Jesus of Nazareth saying to you and to me, to the instruments of the law about that dangling fellow, 'Well done, thou good and faithful servant!' "—*Nashville Tennessean and American.*

ABOLISH PENALTY OF DEATH.

By a vote of 8 to 3 the Judiciary Committee of the House Monday afternoon recommended for passage the Gilbert bill, House bill No. 235, abolishing the death penalty for all crimes in Tennessee. This action was taken following a short address by Duke C. Bowers and a powerful presentation of the objections to capital punishment by K. T. McConnico, of the Nashville bar, and was taken on motion of Lee Winchester, of Shelby, who himself had a bill before the House, leaving the death penalty in effect for rape. Speeches against the bill were made by Representatives Chamlee, Creswell and Bryant, who were the only members of the committee opposing it.

Mr. McConnico's argument, which was so remarkable that it actually convinced men who had made up their minds the other way, was devoted almost entirely to the legal aspects of the case.

He based much of it upon reported cases in which actual confessions had revealed, after men had been executed upon circumstantial evidence, that they were innocent. He had with him a volume of 550 pages filled with such cases, and while he referred to only a few of them, the presence of such a volume, which only covered the cases up to 1901, was in itself a tremendous argument for the passage of the bill.

"The main objection to capital punishment from the lawyers' standpoint is the liability of judicial murder, of mistaken execution through the honest mistake of the courts and juries. This book here is the graveyard of only those cases we know about. How many others there are which have never come to light no man may say."

The most powerful case cited by Mr. McConnico was the Durand case, from California. Durand, ably defended by Delphine M. Delmas, who afterward defended Harry K. Thaw, was convicted of the murder of his sweetheart in the tower of a church on what appeared, so far as human eye could tell, to be an absolutely perfect and unbreakable case of circumstantial evidence, and executed. One year later the pastor of the church in which the murder occurred confessed the murder, when it was too late.

"And yet," said Mr. McConnico, "we must use circumstantial evidence in criminal cases. Were it otherwise, all a man would have to do to go free would be to get his victim off by himself."

"Fifty per cent of the acquittals in homicide cases are due to capital punishment. I am speaking now from my experience in defending half a hundred homicide cases. I know that in cases where the lawyer knows there will be no hanging, he lays his plans from the beginning and fights to convince the jury that the case is 'either hanging or nothing.' The jury naturally revolts at hanging the man, and acquittal results. I have profited by that myself.

IN TENNESSEE.

"Capital punishment increases crime, for the state sets the example of taking life. Not to go so far from home or so far back as the days in England when men were hanged for 300 crimes, in the State of Tennessee, in 1858, men were still hanged for burglary, robbery and arson. Do we have more of those crimes now that capital punishment for them is done away with?"

Mr. McConnico took up the arguments of those who base their opposition to the bill on the pardoning power of the Governor. One class, he pointed out, objected to it because the Governor could, through the exercise of the pardoning power, correct errors of the courts, while the other objected on the ground that the Governor would have power to overturn the decrees of the court. Mr. McConnico criticised both views, citing law and experience on his side.

In regard to mob law, he pointed out that hanging does not prevent the horrible crime for which lynching is committed in the South, but that capital punishment really increases lynching by furnishing an excuse for it, on the ground that the state would take life. "We have all the lynchings that we can have or are going to have as it is," he added.

Two impressive facts were brought out in Mr. Bowers' speech for the bill, that homicide in six states which have abolished capital punishment is only 48 per cent what it is in the capital punishment states, and that back in England two such great authorities as Lord Elgin and Lord Ellenborough predicted ruin and increase of crime if the death penalty was removed from petit larceny.

At the close of Mr. McConnico's speech Mr. Winchester, expressing his conversion and conviction, moved the passage of Mr. Gilbert's bill. Other members of the committee speaking for the bill were Mr. Gilbert and Albert E. Hill, who stated that years ago he had three times voted against a similar bill, but that he now realized that he had made a mistake in so doing.

Mr. Chamlee and Mr. Bryant opposed the bill, particularly as it removed the death penalty for rape, and Mr. Creswell opposed it on the ground that it removed the protection from crimes of violence. He cited the whitecappers of Sevier County, who, he declared, had been checked only by the execution of two men. Mr. Fuller somewhat took issue with Mr. Creswell on this point, maintaining that the man really responsible was never punished.

The final vote of the committee follows:

For the bill—Bejach, Collier of Sumner, Fuller, Abernathy, Neely, Taylor of Jefferson, Williamson, Winchester.

Against the bill—Creswell, Chamlee, Bryant.—*Nashville Tennessean and American.*

EX-WARDEN SAYS "DON'T HANG."

"Relative to the bill now pending before the Legislature to abolish capital punishment for any crime I wish to say that I heartily endorse it and think the stand and work of C. C. Gilbert, Duke C. Bowers and others in endeavoring to effect the abolition of capital punishment is highly commendable," said B. M. Rice, former Warden at the main state prison, talking with a reporter for The Democrat. "After having been connected with the state penitentiary for twenty years, I feel fully warranted from this long experience and close touch with the criminal class that any man of whatever vicious or criminal disposition can be cured under the rigid discipline observed by the officers of the state. The rules imposed upon prisoners school them to such obedience that their conduct necessarily becomes changed from their former life. The mind meets these conditions and accordingly the influence of such environments changes the criminal disposition.

"Under the merit system of commutation of sentence over

seventy-five per cent earn this and not one per cent of the remaining twenty-five per cent are convicted of offenses of such nature that could have resulted in capital punishment—that is, they are not capital crimes. The twenty-five per cent spoken of as not meriting commutation are, as a rule, convicted of minor offenses.

"The record also shows that after a convict has served ten or twenty years and has been released, he becomes a law-abiding citizen, as a result of the rigid discipline imposed while in prison. The practice of capital punishment was not inaugurated under the old barbaric teaching of an eye for an eye, but solely as a protection to society. It is not to punish the offender. No man wants the blood of his fellow-man on his hands, nor should I think he would want it on the hands of his State, of which he is a citizen.

"The responsibility of the State is merely the responsibility of its citizens. Are you willing to assume this responsibility?

"Capital punishment is not a deterrent to crime. I have known of murder being committed almost under the shadow of the gallows. The rapist never reaches the hand of the law. The assassin who lies in wait to kill reasons at the same time that this concealment will avoid the discovery of his connection with the crime. If capital punishment does not deter further crimes and is not a protection to society in this respect, then confinement for life in prison meets every demand of a Christian world."—*Nashville Democrat.*

HITS CAPITAL PUNISHMENT

"I am heartily opposed to capital punishment," said Dean A. B. Martin of the Cumberland Law School, talking with a reporter for The Democrat.

"It does not carry out the true aims of justice—the deterring of the crime. Crime, to a large degree, is a disease, and should be treated as such. When capital punishment takes place there is no opportunity for reformation.

"I am further opposed to capital punishment because man is not infallible. Mistakes are occasionally made, which, under the present system, cannot be rectified.

"Finally, I am opposed to capital punishment because no man has a right to take what he did not give."—*Nashville Democrat.*

CAPITAL PUNISHMENT.

To the Editor of The Banner:

How a Christian minister, who has spent his life attempting to preach Christianity, can favor capital punishment is a mystery to me. To cut the murderer off, believing that he is doomed to eternal punishment, seems to be committing the same crime that the murderer did, and perhaps he did it in the heat of passion, while state does it deliberately.

When Cain slew Abel, God was the only arbiter between men. He was both the political and moral governor of men. Did God kill Cain? No; he gave him a life sentence. A fugitive and a vagabond shalt thou be, and when thou tillest the earth it shall not yield her strength, and added, in order to prevent another murder, whosoever slayeth Cain vengeance shall be taken on him seven-fold. Lamech also, one of Cain's descendants, said to his wives: I have slain a man to my wounding, and a young man to my hurt. If Cain shall be avenged seven-fold, truly Lamech seventy and seven. God, who was all-wise and merciful and changeth not, was not then in favor of capital punishment. Lamech confessed to murder, and Cain denied it.

When a man commits murder his own conscience is a continual tormentor while he lives.

When the state hangs a man she sets a bad example to her citizens, and need not expect any better of them. Would it not be far better to let a murderer be a servant to the state the balance of his life, and give the proceeds of his labor to the bereaved ones of the murdered man?

Think of eternal punishment! Has the state or any individual a right to send any one there? I can hardly see how Lazarus could be so happy while he saw Dives and heard him calling for water to cool his parched tongue. And how ministers now can favor sending their fellow-men to hell does not agree with the teachings of Christ who said: 'I say unto you that ye resist not evil. If thine enemy hunger, feed him; and if he thirst, give him drink; for in so doing thou shalt heap coals of fire upon his head."

Now, was he only talking to his chosen twelve and allowing all other to resist evil? This seems ridiculous; the New Tes tament was given to the world of men. When Cain slew his brother would have been the very time for God to set an example of capital punishment, if he had thought it best.

J. H. OGILVIE.

104 Neil Avenue, Nashville, Tenn.

JOEL B. FORT ON CAPITAL PUNISHMENT.

To The Editor of The Democrat:

The article of Dr. G. A. Lofton in Tuesday's Banner causes me to come forth and make reply for the simple reason that such sentiment as therein expressed by so good and devout a man should not go unchallenged.

That the laws of the Bible are bloodthirsty no one will deny; that the rule of life for life prevailed then goes without dispute; but the question is not whether they were laws then, but should such laws prevail now?

If we are to be governed by the law of life for life, why not also follow the rule of its execution? God gave the law, so the Bible says, and told the Jews how to execute it.

Cities of refuge were set apart, and when a man committed murder and outran the "avenger" and got in the city of refuge safely, then he could have a trial; otherwise the avenger was to kill him. Does any one think such a law just or right? How many offenses were punishable with death? Just think of the horror of it. If a man and woman were caught in adultery it was not a trial and death, but they were stoned to death by a mob. If a man's wife thought to change her religion and worship any other God but the God of the Jews her husband was directed to kill her. I might go at length into the horrible details of those old Jewish laws, but it is not necessary. Our own ancestors brought a list of death penalties to this country that would shock the sensibilities of an average Tennessean—put a man in jail for preaching anything but the orthodox theory of religion, had to go about on Sunday with a look of sanctity that was frightful and forbidden to kiss his wife or babe under penalty of the law.

Times have changed and laws to be wholesome and beneficial must be changed to suit the times.

I care not what good men may think on this subject. After practicing law in the courts of Tennessee for thirty years I know that today human life is held more sacred than at any time in all the history of the world. So true is this that it is hard to get a jury that favors inflicting the death penalty.

Talk of England and her enforcement of the law, it has been but a few score of years since there were more than a hundred offenses punishable with death, and for years it was a nation of king and queen killers, and the laws there are no better enforced than here if you consider the difference in the population. That is an old, settled country, and immigration in that land is all emigration; from all lands come the lower classes to this country, and of course we have a harder criminal proposition to deal with.

There is only one justification for taking the life of an individual in our law, and in the great heart of justice as enthroned in the present day civilization, and that is in necessary self-defense. When the State kills a man, does she do it in necessary self-defense? That is the great question. I don't suppose I am as good a man as Dr. Lofton, but as weak and imperfect as I am, there is nothing that so saddens and horrifies me as all the circumstances and details that are enacted from the Criminal Court to the hangman's noose, an unfortunate creature with the day and hour set for his execution, manacled and carried to the dungeon, with all the blood of his victim red on his hands and reeking and rankling in his heart. Ministers are sent for to aid him in his preparation for his last long journey. They open the Book and tell him of the two roads, one leading to a blissful, eternal life, and another leading to eternal hell fire and torment. He has got to take one or the other, and always takes the heavenly route. A few days of singing and praying and then the fatal hour, and he is consoled by the good men while the black cap is fastened over his eyes and he is sent shooting into eternity.

How a Christian man can see that this method of punishment is just and Christian-like passeth my understanding. If the wolf is not all out of humanity, and they still cry for blood incited on by ministers of the gospel of Christ, let them mob the culprit as did the Jews of old, and let the State set the example of reformation by life imprisonment.

But the Doctor says: "Sickly sentimentalism is even trying

to change the penitentiary into a mere reformatory." Now, doesn't that look strange for so good a man to condemn the efforts of all the good people who are devoting time and talent to alleviate the condition of the under-class of society? I have never been a supporter of Governor Hooper, but every time he does anything to relieve the distress of these unfortunates I feel kinder to him. Sickly sentimentalism. Well, I am glad that I am sentimental and I am glad that I have a forgiving heart, for it is written "forgive us our trespasses as we forgive those who trespass against us."

Most astounding of all I see in the article is this:

"Those who rail at capital punishment for those who murder God's image, rail at God, and make Him out a liar and a tyrant of archaic ignorance and stupidity" Now, what do you think of that?

A good man comes to Nashville at his own expense to beg the Legislature to repeal this brutal law of Jewish barbarism, and he, with all the good men, Dr Vance included, are "railing at God and making him out a liar" But the pity of it is that the Doctor sees that we are growing worse all the time, and says, "and yet the twentieth century has not changed human nature one whit. Vice and crime, murder, adultery, divorce, monopolistie robbery, gambling, political graft, the white slave trade, the saloon and assignation house iniquity, maladministration of justice, lawlessness—all this and more is on the increase in the twentieth century."

I am afraid the Doctor is growing too pessimistic, for a truth I can see that the world has grown better in my day. If what he says is true, what profit has been all the efforts of good men and good women? Away with such an idea! We are climbing higher up the mountain and are leaving the putrid bogs farther behind each year. Civilization has declared against war of conquest, and we have no nation which would stand for a moment to see a Joshua go up and murder the people of Ai and plunder and burn for no other motive than because those people defended their homes. _ ?!

The banner of the Red Cross in the hands of Christian women floats on every battlefield, and tender arms are outstretched to every uunfortunate soldier on either side of the contest. It is humanity that calls for help, and it is the glorious spirit of the advancing age of civilization that is everywhere responding.

Physicians are struggling to stamp out the disease that numbers its victims by the thousands, and right in your own city is a home for those who are in the grip of the great white plague. The Governor and the prison officials and good men and women are at work on the convicts in penitentiary, trying to make them better. Consecrated men and women are baring their breast to every danger in every clime, all working for the uplift of humanity; everywhere orphan asylums managed and cared for by patriotic, Christian men and women, old women's homes, old soldiers' homes, pensions for soldiers on their crutches. My! my! I am glad I live in an age of humanity, when there is not so much prating about the tortures of an endless hell of fire and brim stone, and more unselfish labor for the cause of suffering humanity.

The Doctor says further: "Love and law are correlatives · love alone fulfills or keeps the law—it is love that insists on vindicating the law." This kind of logic may well be advocated in his theology, but I fear the Doctor cannot see daylight when he puts his theories in practice in the criminal law of the State. Keep the law from love! Is that the way you expect the law obeyed, just for love, and when a man doesn't love the law he won't keep it, and he outrages a beautiful woman, and then the State from love hangs him higher than Haman.

It is this way: An honest man does not steal because he stands above the law. It does not affect him. The thief is beneath, and if he refrains from theft it is not for love of the law, but for fear of the law. So with murder. I love the life of my fellow-man and do not murder. I am above the law, and all the good people stand above the law and are trying to raise others above it, and they are reaching down and helping those who are in the underworld to a higher plane and to a new and better life; and so the tendency is in prisons to make the culprit an honest and good man. Is this sentimentalism. If it is, God bless all the thousands of sentimentalists who are today fighting for the uplift of humanity!

The minister stands every Sunday and teaches that though the sins of man are "as scarlet" and of the darkest and deepest dye, that repentance will bring forgiveness. So God will even forgive the murderer and save him in the eternal haven of bliss, the wise and merciful and good God who knows the secrets of the heart, will do this, but when it comes to the State of Tennessee, she must not forgive, nor even confine the murderer for life that he may have time to remedy and repent of his evil deeds, but must cry for blood and must send the murderer from this to another world in a disgraceful manner

"And thine eye shall not pity; but life shall go for life, eye for eye, tooth for tooth, hand for hand, and foot for foot." (Deut. xix., Chap. 21.)

Why! I do not believe if one should advocate such a horrible and barbaric law as that one written, it is said, by the direction of God, in this progressive age, on any inquisition for lunacy he would safely land in the asylum for the insane. It is brotherly love now; it is pity for the unfortunate now; it is mercy and charity now; and with such grand and powerful influences coming from these virtues, the world is growing better and is becoming a place where every man can have enjoyment in knowing there is work for him to do in raising the fallen, cheering the faint and ministering to the unfortunate. "Blessed are the merciful, for they shall obtain mercy."   JOEL B. FORT.

Adams, Tenn., February 13.

CAPITAL PUNISHMENT.

(Editorial from the Nashville Banner.)

Mr. Duke C. Bowers, retired merchant, capitalist and humanitarian, has brought into the present session of the Legislature a unique interest apart from politics and not connected with other public matters to which the attention of the solons has been most deeply directed. Mr. Bowers has a deep conviction that the taking of human life is wrong and not to be justified even though it be in the form of legal execution, and he is making a very energetic effort to have the Legislature pass a bill abolishing capital punishment.

The remarkable feature of his work is that it is purely an individual effort and does not come from any humane society or other organization after the manner that such movements are usually fostered. Mr. Bowers makes the impression that he is very much in earnest, wholly sincere, and there can be no doubt that he is altogether disinterested. The nature of the effort would hardly permit an interested motive, and the man behind it is so entirely dissociated with politics that no such motive can be imagined. It is indeed rare that so determined an endeavor is made in behalf of the supposed public good by an individual of his own initiative, and it is this fact that gives Mr. Bowers' exertions in behalf of the bill he has caused to be introduced a peculiar interest. He has at least succeeded in attracting public attention to the measure and has brought about quite a warm discussion of its merits through the daily press and otherwise.

The sixth commandment of the decalogue very plainly says, "Thou shalt not kill." This was given, engraved on stone, directly from God to Moses in the thunders of Sinai, and seems both explicit and imperative, but some liberal translators have made it read, "Thou shalt do no murder," and this seems warranted by the laws laid down in the next chapter. Exodus 21:12, which says, "He that smiteth a man so that he die, shall be surely put to death," and the death penalty is also prescribed for lesser offenses, concluding with the familiar citation, "Eye for eye, tooth for tooth," etc. Still this was under the old dispensation. The language of Jesus, who overthrew the doctrine of vengeance and taught non-resistance of evil, is used to refute it.

This is the manner in which the religious argument on the subject has gone, but the position is presented in practical guise and the gist of the whole matter is, can society adequately protect itself against crime if the terror of the death penalty be not before the eyes of the evil-doer? As Sir Roger de Coverley was wont to remark, "Much can be said on both sides." Much has been said both pro and con, and the arguments are all interesting and enlightening, if not wholly convincing.

This much is certain, the offenses for which capital punishment is prescribed by civilized nations have very much diminished in number, and crimes formerly so punished have not increased under a lighter penalty. It was, for instance, once a capital offense to steal a sheep in England, and more sheep were stolen then than now.

In Tennessee the death penalty is prescribed only for two offenses, murder and rape. Both certainly deserve the utter rigor of the law. It has appeared to many that the law against murder is now too lightly enforced. At least there have been too many who escaped conviction where the crime was flagrant and the evidence convincing. In England and other countries where justice is surer, murder and all manner of homicides are much more rare. It is argued by those who oppose capital punishment that the certainty of punishment rather than its severity prevents crime. ·However that may be, assuredly nothing should be done that would have any tendency to increase homicides in this state. The record of such crimes here is now disgracefully high compared with other parts of the world where the criminal laws are better enforced.

The proposed abolition of the death penalty for rape presents a problem peculiarly incidental to conditions in this section. If it should be abolished lynchings would likely increase. The same might be true in cases of very heinous murder.

Capital punishment is very revolting to refined sensibilities. The world today will not permit the horrible spectacle of a public execution on which in the past gaping crowds made gruesome holiday. The military executions and political death penalties with which history abounds are, it is to be hoped, a barbarism that is entirely past. There can hardly ever be a recurrence of the horrors of the guillotine. Today neither Major Andre, Nathan Hale or Sam Davis would be put to death. The world is advancing to higher thoughts and milder practice in matters of this kind, but the conclusion is not yet fixed that Tennessee can better its condition by abolishing capital punishment.

CAPITAL PUNISHMENT.

To the Editor of The Banner:

In your editorial today, entitled "Capital Punishment," you refer very kindly to me, but I was extremely disappointed when I read on further and found that you do not concur with me in my fight to abolish the death penalty.

Mr. Gilbert's bill to substitute life imprisonment for the death penalty is, to my mind, one of the most important bills before the Legislature. The decision of this body will be to either discontinue this barbarous practice or else in effect say to the judges, juries and officers of this state, you must continue murdering the state's enemies.

You state too few escape conviction. If you will take the trouble to look up statistics, you will find those states that have abolished the death penalty secure, by far, more convictions than do those states which as yet, unfortunately, have not abolished it.

If the abolishment of capital punishment would cause us to have an increase in the number of homicides, then there might be some argument in favor of retaining the death penalty. But no one is able to say whether there would be an increase or decrease. We can, however, take as an example those states that have abolished the death penalty. In those states homicides have not increased. And a fact very much in our favor is that during the year 1909, which is the last one reported by the United States Mortality Statistics, there were more than twice the number of homicides in the states that retain the death penalty than in those states that have abolished it. Now, if such a condition is a mere "happen so," it is certainly a peculiar "happen so." It surely does give us reason to at least be willing to give the life imprisonment proposition a trial.

As regards "lynchings would likely increase." That is another proposition that can only be definitly determined by trying the life imprisonment plan. To my way of thinking, individuals will come nearer having respect for human life by precept and example from the state than by the state's committing murder and at the same time saying to its citizens, "Thou shalt not kill."
If such a thing as the fear of punishment deters rape, it is the fear of the mob and not the fear of the gallows; but I doubt if the fear of the mob or the fear of the gallows, either, ever enters into the heads of those of that vicious class.

Ex-Warden Rice states "that after having been connected with the Tennessee penitentiary twenty years I feel that any man of whatever vicious or criminal disposition can be cured under the rigid discipline observed by the officers of the state." If there is a chance to cure a man, then isn't it a crime to kill him and deprive him of this chance.

If it is a crime to kill, then do we not, as citizens, almost commit a crime if we neglect to raise our voice or make an effort of some kind to try and put a stop to this legalized murdering of our fellow-citizens.

We may not win in this fight, but we shall at least be consoled with the thought that the blood of these poor unfortunate human beings would not be on our hands if it was in our power to sotp it.   DUKE C. BOWERS.

P. S.—A friend told me that Elbert Hubbard says "that so long as the state continues to kill its enemies, individuals are going to continue killing theirs."   B.
Dresden, February 9, 1913.

CAPITAL PUNISHMENT.
(Editorial from The Public, Mr. Louis F. Post, Editor.)

Five men were strangled at a legalized hanging in Chicago last week. The gallows-trap was sprung by the people of Illinois; for it is true, as one protestant writes to his newspaper, that what we as citizens require of the Sheriff, in conformity with the law upon our statute books against which we make no protest, nor any attempt to alter or abolish it, we do ourselves—all of us and each one of us.

Not many reasons appear for perpetuating these barbarous laws. One of them is that the hanging of murderers is neces sary as a deterrent of murder. The weakness of that excuse is well illustrated in this very case. Swift and relentless was the law's execution, and notorious the fact. Yet "hold-ups" with deadly weapons, the very crime in committing which those hanged men had resorted to murder as an incident, were perpetrated on an ambitious scale (and under circumstances which made murder almost an incident in one and within the intention of the criminals in both) twice within forty-eight hours after these horrible executions and within the sphere of their influence. Legal homicides do not prevent those that are illegal. The former foster the latter, if there is any influence. So completely is this indicated by experience with both, that it is difficult any longer to consider the contrary contention as at once in good faith and intelligent. As an argument it has become only an excuse for that real motive for capital punishment which is rooted in the spirit of revenge—an eye for an eye and a tooth for a tooth. If the vicious spirit of revenge were exercised, and love for morbid excitement were given vent through some less brutal sport, all arguments for capital punishment as a preventive of crime would be abandoned.

The sentimentality which pities the murderer on a gallows regardless of his crime, is bad enough to be sure; but the sentimentality which hangs him out of pity for his victim is worse. If the one is spineless, the other is revengeful. Never should it be forgotten that the great fact which tells against capital punishment is not that it is a disagreeable experience for the murderer, but that where tolerated it is degrading to the community both individually and collectively.

STATES OBJECTION TO DEATH PENALTY.

J. E. McCulloch, General Secretary of the Southern Sociological Congress, has written the following reply to a query by Duke C. Bowers as to his stand on the question of capital punishment:

"Dear Mr. Bowers: I hasten to reply to your query in regard to my ideas on capital punishment, and state that I am opposed to the death penalty; first, because it is unworthy and barbarous for a civilized state to practice revenge; second, because statistics do not justify the conclusion that capital punishment deters crime; third, because the state has no moral right to destroy human life—only God, who gives life, has the right to take it; fourth, because the chief function of the state is to save and improve life—whereas capital punishment arbitrarily cuts off all possibility of reform; fifth, because crime at worst is a symptom of social disease rather than simply the result of individual wrongdoing—the real crime is in our social conditions that make it possible for a murderer to be reared at all."—*Nashville Tennessean and American.*

EDITORIAL FROM THE MARTIN MAIL.

All honor to Duke C. Bowers, the man that is not afraid to do things. If the bill to abolish capital punishment in Tennessee does not become a law he has not failed, for the work he has done will be as bread cast upon the waters to return many days hence. He has attracted the attention of the Union in his fight for the uplift of humanity—the abolishing of capital punishment. It has caused men to put on their thinking caps, and dig deep into the history of capital punishment. It is true that there are man that are opposed to the abolition, but there are more, yea, hundreds to one, that favor the abolishing of capital punishment. It is just and right. The old law, "an eye for an eye and a tooth for a tooth," is of prehistoric days—the old Mosaic laws, and none of those hold good today. Why take life—it is murder —whether done by the law or the individual. It is better to forgive them ninety and nine times. Men that in the heat of passion have slain their fellow-man can and will become great and good citizens if given a chance, but with a hangman's noose there is no chance. Man's humanity to man cries out for the abolition of the law. Will the gentlemen from Weakley County and every other county in the state take notice?

During 1909 the average number of homicides committed to the one hundred population was:

Maine	1.1	No capital punishment.
Massachusetts	2.4	Capital punishment obtains.
New Hampshire	1.4	Capital punishment obtains.
Rhode Island	2.6	No capital punishment.
Connecticut	3.9	Capital punishment obtains.
New York	3.8	Capital punishment obtains.
Michigan	2.2	No capital punishment.
Ohio	5.1	Capital punishment obtains.
Indiana	5.3	Capital punishment obtains.
Wisconsin	1.8	No capital punishment.
South Dakota	4.7	Capital punishment obtains.
Colorado	10.7	Capital punishment obtains.

CAPITAL PUNISHMENT.

EDITORIAL FROM LAFALLETT'S MAGAZINE.

"Do you believe in capital punishment?" asked a United Press reporter over the telephone a few days ago. The occasion for the "interview" was that seven men were to meet death in the electric chair at Sing Sing and that two prisoners were condemned to be hanged here in the District of Columbia.

Some way I cannot get accustomed to the fact that the law and practice that prevails in the District of Columbia are so apt to be an example of unenlightenment. They are subject to the revision of Congress, and if there is a place where capital punishment should not exist, it is here in sight of the capital dome.

I do not object to the death penalty because I think it such a terrible thing for the individuals to whom it is administered, provided they are guilty of deliberate murder. Thousands of

innocent people die daily from wrecks, drowning, and catas-
trophes of all kinds, who suffer more. History gives many examples of men and women who have met the headsman with a
jest. And observers say that the average man, when he goes to
his execution usually keeps his nerve, even to eating a good break-
fast. Nature prepares us all for the inevitable end.

But capital punishment is a survival of barbarism and its
existence is contrary to the best thought and practice of modern
civilization. The old idea was that it was humanly possible to
retaliate a crime, and to mete out justice to the criminal; that
penalties of great severity served as a warning and were a
preventative of crime.

It is said we need go back only one hundred years to find
two hundred offenses punishable by death under the English
law. Within twenty years there were seventeen offenses subject to death penalty under the civil code of the United States.
The extreme penalty did not obviate these lesser crimes nor
does it deter murder. In our country today the extremely small
number—something like two per cent I think it is—of executions,
as compared with the number of murders, must give the hardened criminal great confidence in his chances of escape. And
as for those who commit murder in the heat of passion, they
take no thought of consequences; the large number of those who
thus kill, who turn and commit suicide, or give themselves over
to the law, shows how little the fear of death influences their
acts.

If capital punishment is to deter crime it should be administered in its most revolting form and given the widest possible
publicity. Only a few years ago, hangings were witnessed by
thousands of spectators. The practice no longer prevails. The
public is excluded. And whatever deterrent effect there is from
execution, is produced by the filtered newspaper accounts. There
is a growing sentiment against these news features. It is well
recognized that these recitals suggest many crimes where one is
prevented. The substitution of the electric chair for the gallows
was to lesson the horror of capital punishment. In that degree
it diminishes its deterrent effect.

In view of the change in sentiment which demands that executions shall be as private and free from terror as possible, the
only argument that remains for the death sentence, is that it

relieves society of the burden of support of the criminal and, perhaps, that it is easier for one who has committed murder not to have his life prolonged. But this reasoning applies equally to many crimes, for which capital punishment has been abolished—rape, for instance.

Some wardens say that life prisoners, particularly those who have committed murder under extenuating circumstances, who perhaps might never again violate the law, are much less a menace than those habituated to lesser crimes—professionals so to speak.

Broader understanding of the cause of crime and responsibility for it, is tending slowly to revolutionize the plan of dealing with it. The higher authorities recognize that the struggle is social, not individual; that retaliation and retributive justice is impossible and the attempt to administer it, does not lessen the evil-doing. Anyone who stops to think, must realize that a definite amount of punishment cannot be measured out for a specific offence and that there are many long sentences, even life sentences that might be more safely suspended than to permit the habitual offenders—the incurables—to go free at the expiration of terms as fixed by inflexible statutes.

Investigation and experience have proved, what common sense ought always to have told us, that solitary confinement, or worse, promiscuous herding of criminals in idleness and under harsh conditions, makes the savage more savage, and destroys the hope of improving those not wholly degraded.

Humane and scientific conditions in places of detention—sunlight, air, cleanliness, and methods of reformation—regular employment in healthful and varied and useful occupations, with a degree of compensation as an incentive together with indeterminate sentences, boards for pardon, probation, are all indications of the changed attitude of society toward those convicted of violations of the law. Society is beginning to recognize its responsibility for crime and its obligation to at least administer the law so that its operation will not further degrade the offenders. It is wise economy—even though the first cost be somewhat greater—to direct the effort formerly expended in "punishment" of those imprisoned to fitting them to live and to earn a living, so they may return to the world better prepared to cope with temptation and with less likelihood of being a further menace to society.

CAPITAL PUNISHMENT.

Editor Tennessean and American:

In The Tennessean and American of January 29 I see my old friend McKinney and others have introduced a bill in the Senate to abolish capital punishment in Tennessee. I am sure this is a step in the right direction, and will be encouraged, and doubtless will receive the full approval of a majority of the best people of the state. When a child at my mother's knee, being instructed in the cardinal principles that enter into this life, the obedience or the disobedience of which brings light, joy and sunshine, or darkness and shadow in our path, she pointed me to the law of which, which says: "Thou shalt not kill."

Under her guidance I made up my mind in early life that capital punishment was wrong, for if I did not have the right to kill under God's law and also under the laws of my state, then the state did not have the right to deliberately and coolly murder one of her citizens.

Under the law of Moses it was "an eye for an eye and a tooth for a tooth," but we are living in the light of the Christian era, and God says, "vengeance is mine; I will repay, sayeth the Lord God." Under the Jewish law a man was stoned to death for picking up sticks on the seventh day of the week. Now, in the noonday splendor of the Christian dispensation, we may gather all the brush on the Lord's day that we wish to, and we have done no harm and have violated no principle. We are living under the law of love, and should do unto others as we would have them do unto us.

I shall be glad if Mr. McKinney gets his bill through the Legislature and our dear old state will quit murdering her citizens, and let those who commit first degree murder, repent all the rest of their days.

J. C. HUMPHREYS.

Bells, Tenn.

COPY OF A CIRCULAR I DELIVERED TO THE HOUSE OF REPRESENTATIVES THE MORNING OF THE DAY THE BILL TO ABOLISH CAPITAL PUNISHMENT WAS VOTED ON.

ADDRESS BY D. C. BOWERS.

To the Honorable Members of the Senate and House of Representatives of the Fifty-eighth General Assembly of Tennessee:

In your hands today is placed the life and death of the future unfortunates accused of capital offenses in this state.

If you keep the death penalty on the statute books, the judge, the jury and the executioner, if they keep sacred their oaths, have got to follow your edicts.

An ex-sheriff told me he had to hang two men while he was in office; that he was opposed to capital punishment, yet he hanged those men because it was the law.

A present attorney-general of this state, who believes in the enforcement of all the laws made by you gentlemen and your predecessors, says that he prosecutes capital offenses because it is his duty, but he wishes that the death penalty was done away with.

Gentlemen, there would be mighty little chance of any of us getting to heaven if merit was the only route.

If we get there, there will have to be some mercy shown us.

We cannot afford to be merciful to only those who are guilty of the same things we have been guilty of. God Almighty has not been guilty of any of our sins, yet it is to be hoped that He is going to be merciful unto us.

Our sins are as horrible to Him as the criminal's are to us.

Don't you believe as we spare others He will spare us?

Please give this Anti-Capital Punishment Bill your most careful consideration, and ask yourself if you can afford to take the responsibility of voting to retain a law that means the taking of a human life.

You don't want the stain of human blood on your hands, do you?

Most respectfully,

DUKE C. BOWERS.

PENALTY OF DEATH STANDS.

By a vote of 56 to 36 the House of Representatives yesterday afternoon rejected the Gilbert bill to abolish the death penalty in Tennessee, and tabled a motion to reconsider their action. The defeat of the bill in the House means, beyond doubt, that so far as the present Legislature is concerned the death penalty will remain in force, in spite of the vigorous fight waged against it by Duke C. Bowers and others.

The decision of the House was reached after the longest debate of the session, extending through both the morning and afternoon sessions of the House.

The bill was taken up as a special order at 11 o'clock in the morning, and a vote was not taken until nearly 4 o'clock in the afternoon.

Mr. Gilbert, in moving the adoption of the bill, said crime had been on the increase in Tennessee because of lack of law enforcement.

Mr. Raulston declared that the advocates of the bill appealed for sympathy for the criminals.

Dr. Boyer, who as sheriff of Cocke County hung two men, and the only two men ever legally hung in that county, spoke for the abolition of capital punishment.

"Those two men were, like ninety-nine out of every hundred men, poor and without money. That is why I am opposed to capital punishment—the law is not enforced, as it stands, equally upon all classes alike. If there was equal enforcement of the law I would support it. There is a law for the rich and one for the poor."

Mr. Winchester spoke for the bill as a progressive measure.

Mr. Stone, of Lincoln, closed the argument for the bill. His argument was general, covering the entire subject. He attacked the theories in support of the practice, and cited the statistics, showing that one innocent man is known to have been hanged in the United States each three years.

At the afternoon session the discussion of the bill was resumed. Mr. Mullens argued against the bill, and was followed by Mr. Todd, also against the bill.

Mr. Todd declared that the fact that it was difficult to enforce the law was no reason for abolishing it. He attacked Mr. Stone's argument. He argued especially along the line of protection from rapists.

Mr. Wilson, declaring that Mr. Todd had been appealing to prejudice and passion and nothing else, strongly supported the bill.

Mr. Spears made a powerful appeal against the bill. He declared that sympathy for the criminal was obscuring the interests of the state.

Mr. Rickman spoke against the bill, declaring for law enforcement. Doing away with the gallows would add ten-fold to crime, he said.

The previous question was called for and carried.

The bill was defeated—56 to 36. A motion to reconsider was tabled.

The detailed vote on the bill follows·

Aye—Abernathy, Bejach, Boyer, Byrom, Chamlee, Childs. Collier, of Sumner, Dannel, Dorsey, Emert, Fleeman, Fox. Gilbert, Hill, Kirkpatrick, LeFever, Link, Love, Malone, McCormick, McFarland, Miller, of Lauderdale, Mitchell, O'Brien, Park, Parkes, Pierce, Royston, Shaw, Stephenson, Stone, of Lincoln, Taylor, of Jefferson, Walker, Weldon, Williamson, Winchester. Total, 36.

No—Acree, Albright, Argo, Ausmus, Babb, Barnett, Bryant Bullard, Campbell, Cardwell, Cochran, Collier, of Humphreys, Cox, Creswell, Davis, Denton, Drane, Duncan, Dunn, Fisher, Fuller, Gallagher, Green, Harpole, Henderson, Hughes, Hunt, Johnson, of Madison, Johnson, of Shelby, Long, Matthews Mayes, Miller, of Marshall, Moore, Morris, Mullens, Murphy, Myers, Nichols, Quenichet, Raulston, Rickman, Riggins, Roberts, Robinson, Scott, Schmittou, Smith, Spears, Taylor, of Madison, Testerman, Thompson, Todd, West, Wilson, Stanton. Total, 56.
—*Nashville Tennessean and American.*

KILLING OF LAW FROWNED UPON.

The Duke Bower's bill, which he worked so faithfully and so hard for was killed in the House Wednesday, by a vote of 56 to 36, showing conclusively that Tennessee is not ready to join the progressive states of the union. The Senate Judiciary Committee recommended the rejection of the bill in the Senate. Thus flies the hopes of good and true men, who worked indefatigably for the abolition of capital punishment in Tennessee. —*Editoral, Martin Mail.*

REJECTED.

After an arduous and expensive campaign covering the whole time the Legislature was in session from the first Monday in January until the 22d of February, Mr. Duke C. Bowers, of Memphis and Dresden, saw his bill to abolish capital punishment in Tennessee defeated by much larger odds than he was prepared to expect.

Prompted by humanity alone, Mr. Bowers spent several weeks in Nashville working to pursuade members of the Legislature that legal murder is not good for the country, and at one time he seemed considerably encouraged that our law-makers would abolish what he considers but a relic of barbarism and substitute what he considers a more effective means toward the redemption of the bodies and souls of men. All honor to Mr. Bowers who has done as noble and deserving work as though he had carried his point in more legislatures than one. Unselfishly he spent his time and his money laboring for that which he deeply believed would meet the approval of Him who tempers justice with mercy, notes the sparrow's fall and doeth all things well. In view of the fact that the states having capital punishment show the greater number of homicides it seemed to us that a trial of Mr. Bowers' plan might safely be tried in Tennessee.—*Editorial, Lexington (Tenn.) Progress.*

FIGHT NOT ENDED, SAYS DUKE C. BOWERS.

Duke C. Bowers, who was behind the bill to abolish capital punishment in Tennessee, which failed in the present General Assembly, sends the Democrat the following letter·

To the Editor of The Democrat:

It seems a pity to me that presumably good men construe the Scriptures in such a way as to cause them to believe that the state is justifiable in taking a human life. The horribleness of the thing itself is enough to condemn it, regardless of the doctrine of the law of mercy and love as taught by Jesus.

As to whether the world is growing better or worse has nothing to do with the awfulness of hanging or electrocuting a man. He is some mother's boy; he has sinned, that is true, yet to hang him is only doing the worst thing the state can do to him. The crime can't be undone by taking the offender's life; nothing that society can do can heal the wounds of the injured one; hence where is the common sense in making other wounds, in bringing double disgrace on the parents, brothers, sister and possibly wife and children of the offender?

Any man that reads the New Testament knows "for whosoever shall keep the whole law, and yet offend in one point, he si guilty in all." How such a man can feel that he is able to sit in judgment and cast the first stone is something beyond mv understanding.

"There is one lawgiver, who is able to save and destroy: who art thou that judgest another?"

Surely you are too enlightened to feel "God, I thank Thee that I am not as other men."

"Let not him which eateth not, judge him that eateth."

"Love worketh not ill to his neighbor, therefore love is the fulfilling of the law."

"If we love one another God dwelleth in us."

"He that loveth not his brother whom he has seen, how can he love God whom he hath not seen?"

To my mind the following scripture sums up nearly the whole of Christianity, and there is no capital punishment taught in it. Read carefully. "And as ye would that men should do to you, do ye also to them likewise. For if ye love them which love you, what thank have ye? for sinners also love those that love them. And if ye do good to them which do good to you, what thank have ye? for sinners also do even the same. And if ye lend to them of whom ye hope to receive, what thank have ye? for sinners also lend to sinners, to receive as much again. But love ye your enemies and do good, and lend, hoping for nothing again; and your reward shall be great, and ye shall be children of the Highest; for He is kind unto the unthankful and to the evil. Be ye therefore merciful, as your Father is also merciful. Judge not, and ye shall not be judged; condemn not, and ye shall not be condemned; forgive and ye shall be forgiven: Give it and it shall be given unto you; good measure, pressed down, and shaken together, and running over, shall men give unto your bosom. For with the same measure that ye mete withal it shall be measured to you again."

If I am wrong in my fight to abolish the death penalty, then it is wrong to be merciful. If my fight to save the criminal's life is wrong, then the law of love is wrong.

If I myself was without sin then maybe I could see this thing differently, but I am weak; I try to be good, but it looks like the harder I try the worse I fail. Hence my only hope for life eternal is doing good for others, helping the unfortunate and trying to save the lives of misguided men. Therefore my fight to abolish the death penalty is not ended, and the abusive language heaped upon me by some of the opponents to the measure is not going to stop me. "I am not bound to win, but I am bound to be true. I am not bound to succeed, but I am bound to live up to what light I have."

DUKE C. BOWERS.

Dresden, Tenn., February 28.

CPSIA information can be obtained
at www.ICGtesting.com
Printed in the USA
LVOW04s1513310116

473062LV00025B/2872/P

9 781330 063460